P9-CTB-604

TABLE OF CONTENTS

INTRODUCTION:
The American Arbitration Association

The American Arbitration Association is a public service, membership corporation, founded in 1926 to encourage the use of arbitration and other techniques of voluntary dispute settlement. Members include companies, labor unions, foundations and organizations of all kinds, as well as individuals who believe in arbitration. The Association today is the most important center of education, training and research on arbitration. Under its auspices, hundreds of educational programs are presented every year.

AAA's informational program includes publication of three monthly labor arbitration award reporting services, a quarterly journal, a quarterly arbitration law reporting service, a monthly news bulletin for members, specialized pamphlets covering every field of arbitration, and outlines for teaching labor management arbitration and arbitration law courses. Among the materials produced by the Association are labor arbitration films, each dealing with a typical grievance and illustrating procedures for resolving disputes under AAA Rules.

Arbitration is being used to resolve disputes that unions

and companies have been unable to settle in their grievance procedure. It permits the parties to test their positions against the judgment of an impartial arbitrator. It is a process that the parties have mutually selected. In the words of George Meany, "Voluntary arbitration is the essence of freedom."

A healthy grievance procedure can have a profound effect on the way labor and management get along in their day-to-day relations. Arbitration is more than a mechanism for coping with existing problems; it is a moral force, encouraging a spirit of cooperation which makes it possible for companies and unions to resolve their mutual problems without the agony of an adversary process. This book is dedicated to the proposition that the highest calling of mankind is the task of bringing peace and understanding to the human condition.

Arbitration is not only serving an important function in labor relations: it is increasingly being used to resolve a wide variety of community disputes. Systems based upon traditional labor relations models are now being written into agreements involving tenant councils, student-faculty organizations and prison grievance procedures. Here, the National Center for Dispute Settlement of the American Arbitration Association is playing a leading role.

WHAT THIS BOOK CONTAINS

This handbook describes the grievance arbitration process. It should be helpful to anyone involved in a labor arbitration case. The emphasis is on the practical.

The practice of labor arbitration has tended to become more uniform in recent years. Hearing procedures, to a large degree, are patterned on the Voluntary Labor Arbitration Rules of the American Arbitration Association. This book tells how to proceed under these Rules. It also includes advice based on the AAA's experience in administering over 50,000 labor cases. The Voluntary Labor Arbitration Rules are printed in full, as are the Expedited Labor Arbitration Rules, which provide a "fast-track" service for appropriate cases.

The AAA encourages parties to use arbitration as a problem-solving technique. Again, a practical approach is emphasized. Labor arbitration can be prompt and inexpensive. This handbook contains recommendations as to how parties can reduce cost and delay in their arbitration cases. Your primary interest may be how to win your case; but parties have a mutual interest in using arbitration positively, to eliminate unnecessary conflict. Usually, the spirit of cooperation between management and the work force is more important than transient victories in arbitration cases.

An important section describes some of the factors that should be considered when selecting an arbitrator. The selection procedure may vary, depending upon the language of the arbitration clause in the contract and the desires of the parties; but certain criteria should always be kept in mind. Nothing is more critical than picking the right arbitrator for your case.

Every activity accumulates its own jargon. Labor arbitration, too, requires an understanding of some basic technical words. This handbook contains definitions of those words.

Labor arbitration exists within a legal framework. The leading court cases on arbitration have been described in a brief supplement. The text of the Federal Arbitration Act is printed in full.

Since 1959, the American Arbitration Association has published a monthly *Summary of Labor Arbitration Awards*. It supplements this basic publication with two specialized public sector summaries: *Arbitration in the Schools* and *Labor Arbitration in Government*. As a by-product of these publications, the AAA has compiled a comprehensive index of the issues that have been resolved in labor arbitration cases. The index contained in this book is a valuable research tool. Also included is a bibliography of arbitration literature prepared by the staff of the Lucius R. Eastman Arbitration Library.

This publication contains information that you will want to have in your hip pocket when preparing to discuss a grievance, participating in grievance procedures, or presenting an arbitration case. We think that if you follow the suggestions in this handbook for designing grievance procedures, it will help you settle your cases.

If further information is needed about labor arbitration, inquiries should be made to any AAA regional office. A list of these offices can be found on the back cover. The AAA regional staff help people to use arbitration, providing advice and information about procedures and about individual arbitrators.

Books, pamphlets, films and cassette lectures on arbitration are also available from the AAA. Speakers and complete educational packages can be provided, either through the Education Department of the AAA in New York or through its National Center for Dispute Settlement, located in Washington, D.C.

Individuals or organizations wishing to receive current information on labor arbitration can subscribe to particular services, or can become participating AAA members. The AAA is a public-service organization, created for the sole purpose of helping parties to resolve their disputes through voluntary, non-governmental methods. Members have first call on all AAA educational services, they receive many of the publications on a regular basis, and they receive discounts on books, films and training programs.

CHAPTER 1

SO YOU HAVE A LABOR GRIEVANCE?

During recent decades, labor grievance and arbitration procedures have been adopted by both labor unions and employers as the primary method for resolving collective bargaining contract disputes.

Millions of Americans participate in these procedures as grievants, witnesses, advocates, arbitrators, or as persons affected by the decisions. Whether they are on the side of labor or on the side of management, or serving as impartials, they must have a firm understanding of the process. A few advocates and arbitrators specialize in labor arbitration: most participants arbitrate infrequently, and when they do, they often need to refresh their knowledge of the fundamentals. This guide was written in an effort to help such people by bringing them up to date on labor arbitration.

What follows is a step-by-step description of how labor grievances are handled in arbitration.

Each grievance is unique, depending upon the language of the particular collective bargaining contract, past practices between the parties, and their present relationships. The facts of each case will be different. Some situations may be relatively unimportant to the union or to the employer. Other grievances may probe vital interests of the parties, threatening the power of the union, important rights of individual employees, or the profitability and even the existence of the company. Being a human system, the grievance and arbitration process in action displays all of the foibles of the individuals involved. The sheer variety of potential human conflict lends drama to the practice and handling of these hundreds of thousands of industrial grievances.

In spite of such differences, there are common threads running through the grievance and arbitration practices of collective bargaining contracts, so that a description of customary procedures will be useful.

READ YOUR GRIEVANCE PROCEDURE

The grievance and arbitration provisions of the collective bargaining agreement are interrelated. Only the hardiest grievances are likely to be arbitrated. Before the parties go to arbitration, the grievance will have endured a series of discussions and negotiations, during which both sides should have made a serious effort to resolve their problems. In a healthy relationship, fewer than 10% of the union's grievances have to go before an arbitrator for decision. If a higher percentage have to be arbitrated, something may be wrong with the relationship, and the parties should be concerned.

Union officials have an opportunity to screen out many cases. Some cases need never have been filed as grievances. Others can be withdrawn—or settled. The lost case is a drain on the union. Arbitration can be expensive. A lost case reduces the credibility of the union. On the union side, responsible restraint will build a better batting average and will serve the interests of all the members.

On the other hand, an analysis of the situation may indicate that employer representatives are inflexible in their handling of employee complaints. A harsh personnel policy will often generate unnecessary grievances.

Where representatives of the parties are wasting too much time contesting grievances and processing labor arbitrations, joint discussions at a higher level can be held in order to identify the reasons for the situation and to resolve them. Help from an impartial systems expert can sometimes be useful in this effort.

There are many kinds of grievance procedures. Some are relatively simple; others are far too complicated. You should scrutinize your contract carefully to determine whether the grievance provision is appropriate for your needs. Each step should be tested, particularly as it has been used in practice. Does each step resolve an appropriate percentage of grievances?

Is the procedure self-executing? The moving party should be able to activate the various steps without having to go to court. The grievance and arbitration procedure in the collective bargaining contract is intended to avoid the need for litigation, with its delays, expenses and anxieties. The purpose of the grievance procedure is to enforce the contractual obligations of the parties, establishing employment conditions consistent with the terms of the collective bargaining agreement. Going to court is a sign of failure. In fact, a very small percentage of labor grievances result in any kind of litigation. Court cases are the exception.

At the same time, it should be recognized that the

grievance procedure is an adversary process. Some conflict is inevitable in any complex, changing relationship. The challenge to both parties is to develop systems for the creative management of industrial conflict.

THE LANGUAGE OF THE CONTRACT

Parties should be certain that their grievance and arbitration system is tailored to their needs. These provisions take many forms. Both parties should satisfy themselves that their own arrangement is rational and appropriate.

The arbitration provision should also be reviewed. Is the arbitration clause self-executing? Does it give the moving party the unilateral right to initiate the grievance and to place it before an arbitrator? Or can procedural impasses force the parties into court? Thousands of labor arbitration clauses come to our attention. Many are inadequate, offering ample opportunities to disrupt the procedure. How about yours?

By referring to an administrative agency in the clause, parties can protect themselves—provided AAA is authorized to do more than merely appoint an arbitrator. If one of the parties refuses to arbitrate, the use of AAA Labor Arbitration Rules guarantees that the grievance can be placed before an arbitrator. For example, under Rule 12 of the Voluntary Labor Arbitration Rules, the AAA is authorized to appoint an arbitrator if the parties are unable to agree on one. If it is impossible for the parties to arrange a hearing date, the arbitrator can fix a time and place for the hearing under Rule 19. Nor should there be delay after the hearing. Under Rule 37, the arbitrator must render his award within thirty days after the hearing is closed. If he fails to do so, the AAA must obtain a waiver from both parties. A system of arbitration that is quick, economical and effective can be an important benefit to both parties. Such a system can be obtained by providing for AAA administration in the contract.

Arbitration agreements often represent an intentional compromise based upon the parties' relative bargaining strength, political considerations and other practical needs. The judgment of negotiators may be reflected in nuances in the arbitration procedure. But this is not always the case. Arbitration clauses are sometimes written into the contract in the final rush of bargaining. Beware! The grievance and arbitration provisions should be a thoughtfully-considered part of the bargaining procedure. It should be designed with care.

Arbitration is most often used to enforce the rights of union members. But either party may feel a need to clarify the meaning and application of the contract. Then, the arbitration clause becomes the mechanism under which the matter can be submitted to an impartial expert for a mutually binding decision.

The arbitration clause has an impact upon the parties' behavior. Management actions affecting the interests of union members are subject to the union's right to arbitrate. And, under many clauses, union positions, contested by the employer, may also be subjected to arbitration. The availability of arbitration has a tendency to mold the actions of both parties towards fairness and accountability. The arbitration clause creates "contractual responsibility" between the parties. It forces both parties to abide by contract obligations, in a true spirit of mutual self-regulation.

ARBITRATION IS PARTICIPATION

The grievance and arbitration process requires the involvement of many persons in both organizations. It is a participatory system. As a result, training and orientation is needed so that everyone can understand and make best use of the process. Not only must the official representatives of the parties be well versed as to their rights and obligations under the contract, they must also be able to explain those rights and obligations to their associates. Part of that story is how to use the grievance and arbitration system. Training in skills and techniques is needed.

Management training organizations and international unions provide advocacy training for their own representatives. In addition, impartial organizations like the AAA provide labor arbitration seminars during which representatives of labor and management are exposed to the thinking of experienced labor arbitrators. Hearing procedures, arbitrability, substantive issues such as discipline and discharge, management rights, seniority and other practical problems are discussed by leading experts. One cannot overemphasize the importance of training participants to understand the purpose and techniques of labor arbitration.

It is particularly important to create a positive approach. Here, the responsibility shifts to the top leadership of the organizations involved. Arbitration should be used as a problem solver. It should not be abused. Unnecessary grievances should not be permitted to overburden the arbitration process. Nor should the parties create barriers to a fair hearing. They should avoid having to take their disputes to court. The AAA urges parties to act responsibly. Labor arbitration should not be total war, even though it is an adversary process. Maintaining a healthy relationship between the parties is usually more important than winning a particular case.

MAKING GRIEVANCE ARBITRATION WORK FOR BOTH PARTIES

In the United States, collective bargaining has flourished as a method for working out the arrangements between labor unions, on behalf of the workers they represent, and employers, on behalf of the other participants in the enterprise. The national labor laws have encouraged this process. For disputes such as the interpretation of the collective agreements that result from bargaining, unions and employers have been encouraged to create mutually acceptable procedures, which have usually taken the form of joint discussions terminating in arbitration.

Grievances and arbitration procedures are found in most collective bargaining contracts. Hundreds of thousands of labor disputes concerning the contract rights of union workers have been resolved in this way, without any need for government intervention.

In spite of various wage controls and a pattern of government regulation under the auspices of the National Labor Relations Board and other government agencies, collective bargaining continues to flourish. Labor arbitration is still the instrument of choice for resolving labor grievances. But how long will such a private, voluntary system survive?

There are symptoms of distress. In recent years, discontent has been expressed by the representatives of local unions at several international conventions. Critical articles have appeared. Is the labor arbitration mill grinding too slowly? Is arbitration becoming too expensive? Is the system responsive to the needs of the individual worker?

As an impartial agency, the AAA encourages parties to make arbitration work more responsibly, more efficiently and at less cost.

If parties would exercise restraint in bringing grievances to arbitration, substantial savings could be achieved. Many cases are arbitrated unnecessarily. Union representatives must try harder to screen out the "losers." The AAA's modest filing fee may help union officials to exercise such responsibility. Only bona fide cases are likely to be filed where such a fee must be paid.

The $50 administrative fee charged to each party by the AAA for providing administrative services helps to restrain the filing of marginal cases. In the long run, such a fee benefits the members of unions as well as employers. No one's interest is served by the filing of an unnecessary arbitration claim. Under some arbitration systems, many grievances are filed without any expectation that they will ever go before an arbitrator. This is less likely under AAA procedures. Over 80 per cent of cases filed with the AAA actually proceed to the appointment of an arbitrator.

The arbitrator will generally conform to the arbitration procedure adopted by the parties. It is the parties' responsibility to adopt sensible administrative practices. They should consider ways to make their procedure more satisfactory. Both unions and employers should have an interest in expediting their grievance and arbitration machinery. They should persuade their representatives not to load arbitration with unnecessary costs or inappropriate procedural steps.

Here are some points to bear in mind:

STIPULATIONS AND PRE-PLANNING

One way to reduce delay in the arbitration process is to agree in advance as to the issues. Time is often wasted at hearings because the representatives of the parties have failed to do this. In some cases, parties will find it helpful to sit down with an AAA administrator in advance, in an effort to agree upon an agenda for the hearing. Some issues can be stipulated. Arrangements can be made for presenting evidence in an orderly fashion.

DOING WITHOUT A TRANSCRIPT

Frequently one of the parties will be tempted to order a transcript of the labor arbitration hearing. Although this is permitted under the Voluntary Labor Arbitration Rules, it should be done only with reluctance. Not only are transcripts expensive, but they contribute in a number of secondary ways to the total cost and delay of the process. Where a transcript is requested by one party, the other may feel that it needs one as well. The arbitrator will then feel obliged to refer to it in preparing the opinion. Also, the availability of a transcript increases the likelihood that one of the parties will request an opportunity to file a post-hearing brief. In any case, the preparation of the transcript takes time, the reading of the transcript takes time and consequent briefs take time. Transcripts are one of the prime sources of delay and cost in the arbitration process. Wherever possible, the parties should eliminate transcripts from the procedure.

Some parties have been using tape recorders to make a record of the hearing for their own purposes. Also, some labor arbitrators use such devices to supplement their own notes. The tape does not become the official record of the hearing, but it may be a useful technique for helping to recall points that were made or testimony that was introduced, and may reduce the need for official transcripts.

In a few cases, of course, it will be necessary to make a record of the hearing. For example, where the arbitration award may later be reviewed by the NLRB or a Federal District Court under Title VII proceedings, a transcript may serve a useful function in showing what evidence was considered by the arbitrator in reaching his decision. But even in such cases, a comprehensive arbitrator's opinion may serve the same purpose.

WAIVING OF BRIEFS

Briefs are sometimes necessary. But attorneys should remember that a brief will require the arbitrator to spend additional study time.

In a few cases, a prehearing memorandum as to the issues can be helpful in focusing the arbitrator's attention upon the matter before him. But in most situations the same kind of information can best be presented orally. It has not been customary for labor arbitrators to be exposed to the case until they appear at the hearing. Both parties then have an equal opportunity to make their presentation to the best of their ability.

The post-hearing brief is somewhat more frequently encountered in labor arbitration, particularly where one or both of the parties is represented by an attorney. Here, the parties should discuss with their attorney the necessity of such a brief. Unless there are complex legal issues involved, the oral closing statement that is made at the end of the case is usually enough to set the issues before the arbitrator. If briefs are to be filed, further time will be required. Not only will the arbitrator have to spend time reading the briefs, but the impact of the testimony and the arguments will probably fade from his memory. In many cases, the delay required by a brief will actually diminish the impact of the party's advocacy.

ASKING FOR A PROMPT DECISION

The parties can request an arbitrator to render an immediate decision, asking him to prepare an award on the spot, to be followed by a summary opinion. Under the AAA's expedited rules, the arbitrator is given a few days to write his summary opinion. In many cases, this is all the parties need to resolve their problem.

Sometimes no written opinion will be necessary. The decision itself may be vital: the arbitrator's reasons may be less important. Customarily, an arbitrator charges not only for the day of the hearing but also for the time spent preparing his opinion. By eliminating the need for an elaborate opinion, parties can reduce the total cost of arbitration. In other situations, the parties can sharply reduce the arbitrator's total fee by not referring to analogous cases in their closing statements or post-hearing briefs.

Parties are not always enthusiastic about saving time and money in the arbitration process. Their attorneys are often even less enthusiastic. But frequently the parties will recognize that neither party is served if the employees become disenchanted with the system. Both parties should have a mutual interest in expediting the procedure.

Arbitration must conform to its market. The system will operate only as well as the parties permit. Both the union and the employer should try to make arbitration work in accordance with the needs and desires of the workers. The frustrations created by a congested arbitration system tend to poison the employment relationship. The AAA feels justified in calling upon both sides to exercise responsible restraint.

THE EXPEDITED LABOR ARBITRATION RULES OF THE AMERICAN ARBITRATION ASSOCIATION

All of the time and cost savers described above have been utilized in the AAA's Expedited Labor Arbitration Rules, copies of which are available to all companies and unions. These Rules can be written into contracts to cover less complicated grievances; grievances can also be submitted to arbitration under these rules, if both parties agree.

Under the Expedited Rules, hearings will be scheduled within seven days of the appointment of an arbitrator. Unless the parties otherwise agree, there are no transcripts and no briefs. In conventional arbitration, the parties have seven days to select an arbitrator. Under the new procedure, they must give the AAA the power to appoint an arbitrator. In practice, the regional office calls the parties with the names of a few arbitrators who are available to serve on short notice, attempting to make a mutually acceptable appointment. The Rules provide for a single hearing. The award is due no more than five days after the hearing. The Expedited Rules are printed in the appendix. Where used, they will sharply reduce the cost of grievance arbitration.

THE COSTS OF ARBITRATION

The high cost of arbitration can be a problem for some parties. There are practical ways to reduce this cost.

1. One expense is clearly within the control of each party—the time and money spent by the parties and their representatives in investigating facts and preparing exhibits. Streamlining this process reduces the costs.

In complex cases parties sometimes require the help of outside experts, such as time-study engineers or economists. But such expenditures are not necessary in most grievance arbitrations. Very often, by simplifying the presentation of the case, a party can substantially reduce the cost of preparation.

2. Another item of expense, the stenographic record, can also be avoided. As a general rule, arbitrators take their own notes and do not need stenographic records. A transcript is always optional with the parties. In a few particularly complicated cases, stenographic records are sometimes requested by arbitrators. They may also be necessary for parties in the preparation of briefs. But in many cases the transcript can be eliminated.

As we pointed out earlier, a tape recorder may be useful for refreshing one's memory of a case. The quality of such equipment has improved tremendously in recent years. More and more arbitrators are learning to use portable recorders.

When a party does require a stenographic record, the AAA arranges to have a reporter present at hearings. The party or parties ordering a record will be billed directly by the stenographer.

3. The third item of expense is the fee of the arbitrator. The charges made by arbitrators usually range from $100 to $250 per day of hearing and per day of study time required for the preparation of the award. Under AAA practice, the rate of compensation is agreed upon in advance. Along with the arbitrator's fee there may be reimbursement for travel,

hotel and incidental costs. Often we see parties using the services of distant arbitrators, in preference to equally qualified arbitrators from their own area. Why? There are good arbitrators available in every part of the country. The AAA administrator knows who they are and whether they are available.

Parties should always realize that multiple hearings, briefs, transcripts and citations of cases can add to the arbitrator's fee by increasing the time the arbitrators must spend on the case.

4. The fourth item of expense is the fee of $50 which each party pays to the AAA. For this sum, AAA performs the administrative work in connection with the selection of the arbitrator, the scheduling of hearings, administration and general supervision of the case. This fee pays most of the administrative costs of the AAA in handling labor cases.

By using the Expedited Labor Arbitration procedures, available through all AAA offices, the parties can substantially reduce all of the above costs. And even if the case is administered under the traditional Voluntary Labor Arbitration Rules, the participation of the AAA in the process will ordinarily facilitate the matter, resulting in substantial savings and guarding against procedural impasses that might otherwise require resort to the courts.

ARBITRATORS' FEES

Only part of the increase in arbitration costs can be traced to labor arbitrators' fees. There has been a modest rise in per diem rates. But AAA statistics disclose that the arbitrators have been charging for less study time on AAA cases. In recent years, the ratio between hearing days and study days has declined.

During the past few years, the average cost per hearing day for the arbitrator has increased, but at a rate substantially less than the cost of living or the increase in fees of other professionals.

Labor arbitrators are acutely aware of the need to charge a reasonable fee. Arbitration is a unique profession: after the case, the arbitrator has to collect half of his fee from each party. Losing parties are not likely to show gratitude to the arbitrator who held against them. If arbitrators were charging unreasonable fees, they would have difficulty collecting them; but this is seldom a problem.

The best control mechanism available to the parties is to be sure that the arbitrator is doing productive work during the time that he is being paid. Hearings should begin promptly in the morning and continue throughout the day, with a short break for lunch. Wherever possible, the matter should be completed at the first hearing. Most labor arbitrators are willing to stay late at the hearing if they can avoid the need for a subsequent session.

USING THE MORE AVAILABLE ARBITRATORS

Many of the most acceptable labor arbitrators are reaching the final years of their career. Men and women must be found to replace them. Some critics have called the situation a crisis. They urge parties to make do with less qualified arbitrators. This can be dangerous. The ability of the arbitrator determines the quality of the system.

Parties value their right to participate in picking the arbitrator. Grievances are not abstract contentions over the meaning of contract language. They reflect important, practical disagreements between the parties. Often, the selection of the arbitrator will determine whether a case can be won. The AAA is well aware of the importance of the selection process.

It has been suggested that the supply of available arbitrators be augmented with young apprentices. The AAA does not favor that approach. Labor arbitration requires expert arbitrators. The issues are complex. Both experience and knowledge are needed to decide them.

The advocates have a difficult task. They need an arbitrator who will award in their favor. They also need a decision that is constructive in that it maintains a healthy employment relationship. There are never enough such arbitrators to satisfy the needs of both parties. This is a hardrock fact that confronts arbitration reform.

The AAA believes that many infrequently used arbitrators are qualified. It hopes to increase their use by increasing their visibility. The names and qualifications of such arbitrators are sent out frequently on lists to parties. In addition, the AAA trains qualified labor arbitrators, to replace those who will be retiring in a few years, as well as to lessen the workload on practicing arbitrators.

The solution to the present shortage of impartials is not to flood the market with incompetents. Rather, an effort must be made to gradually bring experienced and acceptable experts into the field. Parties should devote themselves to this task. In the long run, they will benefit from having a larger pool of arbitrators.

POSITIVE APPROACH TO ARBITRATION

Used intelligently and prudently, arbitration will continue to be an effective part of the collective bargaining contract. Not only will it resolve disputes, but it will help communications between union leadership and management, and between the workers and their employer.

Based on ten years of administrative experience in the labor arbitration field, during which over 50,000 labor cases have been administered by the American Arbitration Association, we have come to recognize that arbitration is very much under the parties' direction and control.

Some unions and employers are trying to use badly designed grievance arbitration systems. Others are abusing well-designed systems for irresponsible purposes. These cases are fortunately rare. In most labor relations settings, grievance arbitration is healthy and serviceable. But where breakdowns occur, they tend to discredit labor arbitration. They instill a discontent among the rank-and-file union members, who generalize from the particular—and reject the whole concept.

The labor arbitration community should determine which grievance and arbitration systems are responsible for such discontent. These systems should be analyzed. What are the reasons for their delay, and for unreasonable costs? How could cases be expedited? Which unnecessary steps could be eliminated?

Labor arbitration is still a relatively new institution. It generally is serving its purpose, solving problems for union leaders and for executives. In tens of thousands of contractual relationships, the grievance and arbitration system is quietly going about its business, helping the parties to settle their disagreements.

CHAPTER 2

HOW TO SELECT A LABOR ARBITRATOR

The selection of the arbitrator is very important. The arbitration provision in the contract will ordinarily describe how this is to take place. While participating in the selection process, each party should strive for the best possible arbitrator.

Arbitrators are chosen in various ways. Many contracts contain a reference to the Voluntary Labor Arbitration Rules of the American Arbitration Association. The description here will relate to the way arbitrators are chosen under that system.

A survey of AAA cases indicates many cases in which local unions and employers have only one or two arbitrations during the year. Representatives of such parties find it difficult to become familiar with the relative abilities of individual arbitrators. In contrast, other practitioners constantly engage in labor arbitration, and become well versed as to the arbitrators. A selection process that is appropriate for the experienced labor lawyer may not meet the needs of the novice.

The tripartite system was once popular. Parties now find

it unnecessarily complicated. Union members seem to prefer a system where the entire case is presented openly to one impartial arbitrator. They tend to distrust "executive sessions," suspecting that deals and compromises take place. The trend in grievance arbitration is toward a single arbitrator.

No part of the arbitration clause is more important than how the arbitrator will be selected. The predictability of arbitration depends substantially upon the knowledge, experience and understanding which the arbitrator brings to the hearing. Careful consideration should be given to the selection process set forth in the collective bargaining agreement.

Most labor arbitration provisions guarantee to the parties the right to participate in the selection of an arbitrator. The facts and circumstances of the case and full information about available arbitrators must be carefully appraised by the parties before the selection is made. Hopefully, this process results in an appointment of the best available arbitrator. It is just here that the *ad hoc* system displays its strength.

A technique for suggesting appropriate names to parties in connection with specific cases is contained in the AAA Voluntary Labor Arbitration Rules. This system relies heavily upon the judgment of the tribunal administrators of the twenty-one AAA regional offices.

As the New York State Supreme Court has stated, "The AAA, through a long and active career, has gained an enviable reputation for the absolute impartiality of its conduct in all the various steps and phases of arbitration —so much so that it is commonly designated by the parties in contracts providing for arbitration."

The reputation of the AAA is based substantially upon

the informed judgment of its regional directors and their staff, who keep abreast of the activities of labor arbitrators in their own area. They know which arbitrators are available, and what kind of cases they are best suited to handle. Parties have different needs. The appointing agency must recognize these differences in submitting a list of arbitrators. A small union arbitrating a discipline case against a local job-shop needs a quite different list of arbitrators than would a large union bringing a more complicated case against a national manufacturer. The personal judgment of the tribunal administrator is an important element in satisfying the needs of the parties.

The judgment of an impartial administrator can help the parties in selecting an appropriate arbitrator. Lists of labor arbitrators sent out by AAA offices reflect a professional judgment exercised on behalf of the parties.

Some contracts don't specify what happens if the parties are unable to agree on an arbitrator. In these cases it is sometimes necessary to go to court. However, if both parties are agreeable, a list can be obtained from an appointing agency, since at any stage, parties to a labor dispute can turn to the AAA for help. But it often avoids trouble if the AAA is specified in the collective bargaining contract.

SELECTING THE ARBITRATOR UNDER AAA PROCEDURES

Unless parties have selected a different method, the American Arbitration Association follows the following procedure:

1. Upon receiving a demand for arbitration, the AAA

acknowledges receipt and sends each party a copy of a specially prepared list of proposed arbitrators. In drawing up this list, the tribunal administrator will be guided by the union's statement of the nature of the dispute. Basic information about each arbitrator is attached to the list. Where parties need more information about a proposed arbitrator, the AAA is glad to supply such information on the phone.

2. The parties cross off the unacceptable names, and number preferentially those remaining.

3. When the lists are returned by the parties, the AAA compares them to determine which arbitrator is most acceptable. That arbitrator is then contacted, so that available dates can be obtained. The arbitrator is asked for available dates, and whether there is any reason why he could not act with impartiality in a dispute between the parties.

4. Where parties are unable to reach a mutual choice from a list, the AAA will submit additional lists, but only at the request of both parties. If the parties still fail to agree upon an arbitrator, the AAA is authorized to make an administrative appointment. In no case is an arbitrator appointed whose name was crossed out by either party.

Collective bargaining agreements sometimes provide for tripartite boards of arbitration, without setting time limits for appointment of the party-appointed arbitrators. Even there, the AAA system can be used to give force and effect to the wishes of the parties.

Where the collective bargaining agreement provides for selection of an impartial member of a board of arbitration "by the American Arbitration Association," lists are sent to the parties or to the party-appointed arbitrators, in accordance with the terms of the contract or the wishes of the parties.

ARBITRATOR LISTS

The AAA submits lists in accordance with the particular arbitration clause involved. In addition, the make-up of the list reflects what is known about the past preferences of the parties. The regional office staff know that they are often judged on the quality of the lists that they issue on labor cases.

The AAA serves as an expediting agency, offering to parties those arbitrators who are likely to be mutually accepted and withholding arbitrators who will be rejected. The AAA acts as an agent for both parties, seeking to calculate in advance what kind of arbitrators will be acceptable to both. By having this judgment made by a local representative, a sensitive and informed service can be provided.

All of this effort results in a list of names. Then the responsibility for the selection process shifts to the advocates. What do parties need to know about a particular arbitrator submitted on a list? What information is it useful for the AAA to supply? What must be obtained elsewhere?

SOURCES OF INFORMATION

A copy of each arbitrator's card is mailed out with the list being submitted. Each AAA office is prepared to provide parties with additional, contemporary information about the arbitrator.

This information is only a small part of what the parties

need to know about the arbitrators on the list. They may also want to study recent awards that the arbitrators have rendered, particularly on similar issues.

The AAA publishes a monthly *Summary of Labor Arbitration Awards* which lists hundreds of carefully selected arbitration awards. The service includes over 3,000 cases since April, 1959, the first month of publication. The name of the arbitrator and the issues considered are listed in each case. The names of the parties and the location of the hearing are also included.

This service can be particularly useful to a party wishing to find out what a particular arbitrator has previously written on similar issues. By using the cumulative index, decisions listed for that arbitrator can easily be located. The full text of those opinions which are of interest to him can then be obtained directly from the AAA.

COMMERCIAL SERVICES AND OTHER SOURCES

Other publishers also report arbitration awards. These opinions are acquired from various sources. Many are obtained from opinions filed with the Federal Mediation and Conciliation Service. In addition, publishers sometimes receive labor awards directly from arbitrators. Arbitration awards rendered by permanent umpires are also published.

Several commercial services, catering to management representatives, report the opinions of employers and their counsel who have used a particular arbitrator on prior cases. Subscribers receive such information by paying an annual fee.

Management groups maintain similar clearing houses of information about arbitrators, as do several of the management-oriented law firms. When a member of the network uses an arbitrator, he is asked to fill out a report form which becomes part of the material on file.

In the same way, unions and labor-oriented law firms collect information available to certain union officials. Sometimes, these networks are administered by the education directors of the international unions.

Active practitioners will search out whatever networks of information are available for their use. There are ways to find out what the people on your side think of a particular arbitrator.

EVALUATING AN ARBITRATOR

Information about a particular arbitrator will be obtained primarily from parties who have used that arbitrator on prior cases. What do they say about the arbitrator's ability, philosophy, and impartiality?

Is the arbitrator competent to understand the particular kinds of issues that will be involved in the case? Does he have general competence to sift facts in an adversary procedure? Does he have the engineering or technical background sometimes required on certain issues? Has he had experience in the particular industry? Is he too legalistic or not legalistic enough? Does he have a particular philosophy which would make him suitable for the issues of the case? These are some of the questions that will be asked about the arbitrator who is being selected. The parties are not concerned with making positive or negative judgments of the man's philosophy; they are interested in winning the case.

Evaluating an arbitrator is a matter of opinion; expertise in this area varies from advocate to advocate. Many practitioners believe that their experience and judgment make it possible for them to match the issue to the arbitrator.

One unfortunate by-product of the system is that practitioners become hesitant to accept an unknown quantity. The tried-and-true arbitrators are used again and again. The new arbitrator does not get chosen.

Introducing relatively unknown arbitrators into the process is not easy, although the situation is not as hopeless as is sometimes claimed. New men and women are coming into the profession, and are being accepted. Some are being accepted with surprising speed. Looking at the matter statistically, we do find a fair proportion of relatively young arbitrators. A 1971 survey indicated that 28.2 percent of the 532 arbitrators who served on AAA cases were less than 50 years of age—7.2 percent were under 40.

Since the mechanism for the selection of labor arbitrators is entirely dependent upon the free choice of the parties, mutually exercised, it may be necessary for a significant change in attitude to take place before a flood of new and younger arbitrators enters the field. Fifty or more new arbitrators obtain appointments each year. Some go on to become widely accepted by the parties. A difficult challenge faces them, because the parties are conservative about their selection.

The conservatism of the advocates reflects pressures placed upon union agents and company personnel to obtain arbitrators who will render acceptable awards. The unknown quantity of a relatively new arbitrator is particularly frightening to a person who is under such pressures. It may be necessary for parties to instruct their representatives to take a chance on new arbitrators on appropriate cases. Only thus can the problem caused by a narrow supply of arbitrators be overcome.

For its part, the American Arbitration Association is constantly seeking out new arbitrators and arbitrators already on the panel who are being under-utilized, considering their experience and potential acceptability.

HOW ARBITRATORS GET ON THE AAA PANEL

Over many years, the American Arbitration Association has created a roster of arbitrators for use in all kinds of labor arbitration cases throughout the country. Almost 2,000 labor arbitrators are now on the panel, although most of the work is done by less than 400 active arbitrators. Virtually every labor arbitrator in active practice in the United States is on the AAA list.

How are new names obtained? How are candidates screened by the AAA? And how is the quality of the panel maintained?

The AAA's officers and regional directors constantly search for persons who have a good potential for being accepted as labor arbitrators. Men and women who are being selected on an *ad hoc* basis by parties in their local area are one source of talent. Many arbitrators come from government mediation agencies. Others teach industrial relations or labor law at universities, or have a strong academic background in these fields. We often will encourage a professor with industrial relations experience to file an application to the labor panel. Attorneys or other professionals with a knowledge of industrial relations sometimes achieve acceptability.

Few experienced labor arbitrators serve as advocates for labor or for management. Such service tends to reduce potential acceptability as a neutral. Therefore, advocates are not encouraged to apply to the AAA National Panel.

When a nomination is received from a reliable source, an invitation is usually issued. In a few cases, an initial investigation is made to determine whether it would be a waste of time to process the candidate's application. It serves no good purpose for anyone to recommend that an inexperienced person be invited to apply.

LABOR PANEL DATA SHEET

The candidate is required to fill out a Labor Panel Data Sheet. This document has two parts. One part requires information identifying the candidate, his present and previous business affiliations, professional licenses and education. Information about education and previous employment is requested. But, while most labor arbitrators have a thorough academic background, often including legal training, there are some who have not completed college. Most labor arbitrators have had some prior experience with practical industrial relations, but there are some who have never worked in the field. Many arbitrators are lawyers; almost a third are not. Most lawyer arbitrators do not represent clients in labor relations; some do. In short, the guidelines are far from rigid. Exceptions are found to each of them.

The second part of the Data Sheet may be more relevant. Each candidate is asked to give the names of four union and four management references. Letters to these references produce comments as to the candidate's character and abilities. A few letters repudiate the applicant. Other references, not willing to make critical statements in writing, telephone the AAA and say that they cannot recommend the person who used their names. Sometimes one can read a signal, between the lines, indicating a reservation about a candidate. A frank discussion on the telephone with the writer of such a letter will often clarify the situation.

ADMITTANCE TO PANEL

A candidate may be admitted to the panel on the basis of the application form and letters of reference. The decision to accept candidates is made administratively by AAA staff.

In about one-third of the cases, the reference letters will indicate the need for further investigation. Such investigations are carried out by AAA regional offices, and may result in a decision not to place the arbitrator on the labor panel.

When a person is placed on the panel, a card is prepared which describes the arbitrator's history and background. A copy of this card is sent to those regional offices which are likely to send out the arbitrator's name on lists to the parties. The card of an arbitrator with limited acceptability may be sent to only one office. In other cases, cards may be distributed to several regional offices.

Arbitrators sometimes lose their acceptability. An arbitrator's chronic illness or advanced age may cause parties to distrust his judgment. Sometimes arbitrators encounter temporary personal problems: alcoholism, nervous breakdowns and the like. These problems may require that the arbitrator's name not be submitted on lists.

Where an arbitrator habitually overcharges parties or is unable to arrange a hearing within a reasonable time, AAA offices may stop sending his name out on lists. The AAA's responsibility is to serve the interests of the parties, by providing them with the best possible arbitrators. Sometimes, regional directors will be directed to use such an arbitrator with caution.

In other situations, a regional office will not send out the arbitrator's name on certain types of cases. The AAA relies heavily upon the judgment of its local regional directors, who must weigh the acceptability of each arbitrator on their panel against the needs of the parties in the particular case. The regional office has responsibility for preparing lists for cases, for selecting the best names for the parties and the issues. Regional staff are expected to know their panel members' experience, expertise in special fields, availability for quick service, billing practices, and record of acceptability for particular companies and unions. This knowledge can be converted into a practical benefit to parties when lists are issued on pending cases.

EXPOSING NEW ARBITRATORS TO THE LABOR-MANAGEMENT COMMUNITY

The AAA recognizes its duty to try to help new arbitrators get accepted by the employers and unions that might wish to use them. Often, these arbitrators are fully qualified: their problem is to be better known.

New arbitrators must be introduced to the attention of potential users. This can be done in a number of ways. The AAA's Educational Department sponsors labor-management conferences: new arbitrators are invited to attend so that they may meet some of the practitioners in the field. Awards by new arbitrators are published in the *Summary of Labor Arbitration Awards*, and the other AAA publications.

In several cities, the AAA has cooperated with other agencies in encouraging the use of a selected group of arbitrators. This has been done in areas where there is a shortage of practicing labor arbitrators. Such programs have been carried out in Buffalo, Philadelphia, Cleveland and other cities. Participants accompany more experienced labor arbitrators to hearings and write practice awards. The local labor-management community participates in these programs, getting to know the new arbitrators.

What can a new labor arbitrator do to become more widely accepted in his profession? The arbitrator must be able to perform competently in those cases for which he or she is selected. The arbitrator must become known favorably throughout the labor-management community. This must be done on a personal basis. If possible, an arbitrator should join appropriate professional groups. It can also provide good exposure to publish articles in *The Arbitration Journal* and other recognized publications.

The AAA serves the labor-management community by maintaining an excellent list of arbitrators, by submitting carefully selected lists in accordance with the arbitration clause in each collective bargaining contract, and by introducing new arbitrators whenever they will be used by the parties.

The AAA system assigns personal responsibility for the selection of names to local regional offices. Accurate and objective information as to panel members is supplied by the AAA. The dissemination of subjective opinions as to arbitrators is better left to partisan agencies.

By learning where to turn for information about arbitrators, the practitioner can do a better job of selecting the right arbitrator for the case. Nothing in labor arbitration is more important.

CHAPTER 3

PREPARING FOR THE ARBITRATION HEARING

By the time a case reaches arbitration, representatives of both parties have usually spent many hours discussing the grievance. In these talks, at each level of the grievance procedure, they should have become familiar with all the facts and complications of the matter. If they are unable to agree, both parties face the problem of communicating their understanding of the facts to the arbitrator, who usually knows nothing about the dispute until the hearing begins.

Effective presentation of the facts and arguments must begin with thorough preparation. The following steps are suggested:

1. Study the original statement of the grievance and review its history through every step of the grievance machinery.
2. Review the collective bargaining agreement from beginning to end. Often, clauses which at first glance seem to be unrelated to the grievance will be found to have some bearing.
3. Assemble all documents and papers you will need at the hearing. Make photostatic copies for the arbitrator

and for the other party. If some of the documents you need are in the possession of the other party, ask that they be brought to the arbitration. The arbitrator usually has authority to subpoena documents and witnesses if they cannot be made available in any other way.

4. Interview all of your witnesses. Make certain they understand the theory of your case, as well as the importance of their own testimony. Run through the testimony several times. Role-play the probable cross-examination.

5. Make a written summary of the testimony of each witness. This can be useful as a check-list at the hearing, to insure that nothing is overlooked.

6. Study the case from the other side's point of view. Be prepared to deal with opposing evidence and arguments.

7. Discuss your outline of the case with others in your organization. A fresh viewpoint will often disclose weak spots that you may have overlooked.

8. Read published awards on the issues that seem to be involved in your case. While awards by other arbitrators on cases between other parties are not decisive as to your own case, they may be persuasive. The American Arbitration Association publishes Summaries of thousands of labor arbitration awards in its monthly publications. Use these Summaries and their cumulative index as a research tool.

THE ARBITRATION HEARING

The date of the hearing is fixed by the arbitrator. Usually, the AAA tribunal administrator first consults the parties and then arranges a date with the arbitrator. The administrator then notifies the parties.

The adminstrator will also arrange in advance for a stenographic record of hearings, if requested to do so by one of the parties. Remember that such a transcript is expensive. Do you really need one? How do you plan to use it? If an official transcript is kept, the arbitrator may feel that he has to read it. This may delay his award. It will also increase his total fee.

The customary order of proceedings at the hearing is as follows:

1. Opening statement by the initiating party, followed by a similar statement by the other side.

2. Presentation of witnesses by the initiating party, with cross-examination by the responding party.

3. Presentation of witnesses by the responding party, with cross-examination by the initiating party.

4. Summation by both parties, usually following the same order as in the opening statements.

This is the normal order. The arbitrator may vary it, either on his own initiative or at the request of a party. For example, in discipline or discharge cases, it may be logical for the employer to go first. The order in which the facts are presented does not imply that the "burden of proof" is more on one side than the other. Both parties must try to convince the arbitrator as to their position.

HOW TO PRESENT A CASE IN ARBITRATION

1. **The Opening Statement**—The opening statement should be prepared with care. It lays the groundwork for the

testimony of witnesses and helps the arbitrator to understand the relevance of oral and written evidence. The statement should identify the issues, indicate what is to be proved, and specify the relief sought. Refer the arbitrator to relevant contract provisions. Give the arbitrator ample time to read the language for himself.

The request for relief should be specific. If back pay is demanded, for instance, the complaining party should have computed the exact amount. The arbitrator's authority to grant the requested relief under the contract should be clearly defined.

Because of the importance of the opening statement, some advocates present it to the arbitrator in writing, with a copy for the other side. They believe that it is advantageous to make the initial statement a matter of permanent record. This is a matter of personal style. In any case, an opening statement should be made orally, even when it is supplemented by a written statement. An oral presentation adds emphasis to the argument.

Parties sometimes stipulate facts about the circumstances which gave rise to the grievance. This is a good idea. By giving the arbitrator the uncontested facts at the outset of the hearing, the parties can save time and reduce costs.

2. **Presenting Documents**—Documentary evidence may be an essential part of the case. The collective bargaining agreement, or the sections that have some bearing on the grievance, should always be submitted. Documentary evidence may also include official minutes of contract negotiation meetings, personnel records, medical reports, wage data and relevant correspondence. Every piece of documentary evidence should be identified, with its authenticity established. This material should be physically

presented to the arbitrator (with a copy for the other side). The significance of each document should be explained. In some instance, key words, phrases and sections of written documents should be underlined, to focus the arbitrator's attention on the essential features. Properly presented, documentary evidence can be most persuasive.

3. **Examining Witnesses**—The facts at issue generally are presented through direct examination. After a witness is identified and qualified as to the facts about which he will testify, he should be permitted to tell his story largely without interruption. Leading questions are usually permitted in arbitration, but testimony is more effective when given in the witness' own way. Questions sometimes can be useful in emphasizing points already made, or in leading a witness back to the main line of testimony.

4. **Cross-Examining Witnesses**—Every witness is subject to cross-examination. Among the purposes of such cross-examination are disclosure of facts the witnesses may not have related in direct testimony; correction of misstatements; placing of facts in their "true" perspective; reconciling apparent contradictions; and attacking the reliability and credibility of adverse witnesses. In planning cross-examination, the objective to be achieved should be kept in mind. In most cases, proof can best be presented by friendly witnesses. Sometimes, you may want to waive cross-examination because you believe that it will only serve to reinforce the testimony of a hostile witness.

5. **Maintaining the Right Tone**—The atmosphere at the hearing often reflects the relationship between the parties. While the chief purpose of the arbitration hearing is the

determination of the particular grievance, a collateral purpose sometimes can be achieved: skillful and friendly conduct by the advocates can sometimes create a better relationship between the parties. To this end, the parties should conduct themselves in a dignified manner. The arbitration hearing should be informal, but orderly.

An arbitration is no place for emotional outbursts, long and irrelevant speeches, caustic remarks or personal invective. Apart from their adverse effect on the relationship between the parties, such tactics are not likely to persuade an arbitrator. Over-legalistic approaches are also counter-productive. The arbitrator will usually be a seasoned professional. He is not going to be swayed by bombast or by the jargon of the courthouse.

A party has every right to object to irrelevant evidence: the arbitrator should not be burdened with material that has no bearing on the issues. Objections should not be made merely for the sake of objecting. They may give the arbitrator the impression that you are afraid to let the other side be heard.

6. **The Summary**—Before the arbitrator closes the hearing, he will give both sides an opportunity to make a closing statement. The purpose of this is to summarize the facts and the issues, and to justify the decision the arbitrator is being asked to make.

Arguments may have been injected into the earlier testimony. But often arbitrators require parties to concentrate on presenting evidence, withholding their arguments until the summary. Then, the closing statement is vital. This may be your last chance to convince the arbitrator. Points made by the other side can be refuted at this time.

7. **Post-Hearing Procedure**—After both sides have had equal opportunity to present their evidence and arguments, the arbitrator will declare the hearing closed. Under AAA Rules, the arbitrator has 30 days within which to render the award, unless the collective bargaining agreement contains some other time limit. If parties need to file post-hearing briefs, or additional documents, the arbitrator can set appropriate time limits; hearings remain open until all documents are received. Post-hearing material is exchanged through the AAA tribunal administrator. The parties should not communicate with the arbitrator, except when both sides are present. The AAA will see that the briefs are transmitted to the arbitrator.

8. **How to Reopen Hearings**—When parties jointly agree to add certain data after a hearing is closed, they may arrange to do so by written stipulations filed with the AAA. The arbitrator will then study the new material.

In the event new evidence is discovered, or when a situation arises that seems to require explanation, parties should not attempt to communicate directly with the arbitrator. They should request the arbitrator, through the AAA, to conduct an additional hearing or otherwise arrange for presentation of necessary evidence. An arbitrator may also reopen hearings on his own initiative.

Contact between the parties and the arbitrator should be channeled through the AAA in order to eliminate any suspicion that one side may have offered arguments which the other had no opportunity to rebut. Of course, in some situations, the relationship between the parties will be such that direct contact with the arbitrator will be customary, and appropriate.

TEN WAYS TO LOSE CREDIBILITY IN ARBITRATION

1. Using arbitration as a harassing technique by arbitrating grievances that can't be won.

2. Overemphasis of the grievance by the union or exaggeration of an employee's fault by management.

3. Insufficient preparation, with reliance on a minimum of facts and a maximum of arguments.

4. Introducing witnesses who have not been properly prepared as to demeanor or the importance of their testimony in the case.

5. Unsuccessfully attempting to conceal essential facts or to distort the truth.

6. Refusing to show books, records and other documents, until required to do so by subpoena.

7. Clogging the procedure with legal technicalities.

8. Withholding full cooperation from the arbitrator.

9. Disregarding the ordinary rules of courtesy and decorum.

10. Engaging in a debate with the other side. The time to try to convince the other party is before arbitration, during grievance discussions. At the arbitration hearing, efforts should be concentrated on convincing the arbitrator.

THE AWARD

The award is the decision of the arbitrator upon the matters submitted to him under the arbitration agreement. Its purpose is to dispose of the controversy, finally and conclusively.

The award should be limited to the issues as defined in the arbitration agreement, should rule on each claim submitted, and should be definite and final. Generally, the award is accompanied by an opinion which reviews the evidence and sets forth the reasoning of the arbitrator.

The power of the arbitrator ends with the making of the award. An award may not be changed by the arbitrator, once it is made, unless the parties mutually agree to reopen the case and to restore power to the arbitrator. In legal terms, the arbitrator is *functus officio* after he signs the award.

When the parties do agree to ask the arbitrator to reopen a case in order to obtain a clarification or interpretation of an ambiguous award, the agreement to reopen should be in writing and should set forth precisely the question submitted. When such an agreement is filed with the AAA, the tribunal administrator will make necessary arrangements with the arbitrator.

AWARDS BY TRIPARTITE BOARDS

The use of tripartite boards of arbitrators sometimes creates special problems. Usually, an award must be supported by a majority of the arbitrators. The difficulty is that party-appointed arbitrators often regard themselves as advocates of their sides. Scheduling problems, considerations of cost and the ambiguities of the party-appointed arbitrator's role are convincing most parties to avoid the tripartite board system.

In very important cases, the parties may want to have the benefit of a group judgment, in which case they may wish to agree on a panel of three neutral arbitrators.

APPENDIX

The Jargon of Labor Arbitration: A Glossary

1. ***Ad Hoc* Arbitrator** An arbitrator jointly selected by the parties to serve on one case. Many employers and unions believe that decisions are more likely to be fair and equitable if the arbitrator is chosen on a case by case basis. If both parties are satisfied with the arbitrator's ability, they may select him again for another case. The *Ad Hoc* system enables the parties to retain their freedom of choice.

2. **Adjournment of Hearing** The arbitrator has the power to postpone a hearing until another time, at the request of either party (see AAA Voluntary Labor Arbitration Rule 23). If the arbitrator unreasonably refuses to postpone a hearing, a losing party may have grounds for vacating the award.

3. **Administrative Agency** An impartial private or governmental agency which maintains panels of labor arbitrators. Administrative and appointing services can be obtained by an appropriate reference to the agency in the collective bargaining contract. The AAA is the only private agency in the United States.

4. **Administrative Appointment** The designation of the arbitrator by an administrative agency. Sections 12, 13 and 14 of the Voluntary Labor Arbitration Rules provide for administrative appointments in the event of impasse. When parties have failed to agree on a mutual choice from a list submitted to them, the AAA

may make the appointment. Under expedited arrangements, the parties may empower the AAA to make the appointment without a preliminary submission of lists.

5. **Advisory Arbitration** A system under which an arbitrator is selected to render an award which recommends a solution to the dispute. Advisory arbitration has been used most frequently in public employment, often to help resolve bargaining impasses.

6. **Affidavit** A statement in writing made upon oath, before a notary public or other authorized officer. Such statements are sometimes submitted and received as evidence in labor arbitration hearings. Section 29 of the Voluntary Labor Arbitration Rules states that: "The Arbitrator may receive and consider the evidence of witnesses by affidavit, but shall give it only such weight as he deems proper after consideration of any objections made to its admission." Where the witness is available and could be cross-examined, the arbitrator may refuse to accept such an affidavit.

7. **Appeal** A proceeding for obtaining a review of a decision. In arbitration, the right to an appeal is seldom provided. An award may be challenged in court by a motion to vacate. In labor arbitration, such motions are generally based upon allegations that the arbitrator exceeded his authority.

8. **Appointment of Arbitrators** Arbitrators are chosen by the parties in accordance with the procedures designated in the arbitration clause in their collective bargaining agreement. Most provisions call for the appointment of a single arbitrator. But some agreements still provide for the designation of "party-appointed arbitrators," who then select a single, neutral arbitrator to act as chairman. If the party-appointed arbitrators or the parties themselves are unable to agree upon an arbitrator, a court may make the appointment on the motion of one of the parties. The parties can avoid the necessity of going to court by designating an administrative agency in their contract.

9. **Arbitrability** Does the moving party have a right to arbitrate the dispute? Procedural arbitrability often turns on whether specified steps have been carried out prior to the initiation of the

arbitration. Substantive arbitrability concerns the scope of the arbitration clause. The arbitration agreement should describe the kinds of disputes it covers, and what prior steps must be completed before a party has the right to demand arbitration. Questions of arbitrability may be determined by an arbitrator or in court, depending upon the arbitration provision in the contract and the applicable law. Under Sec. 301 of the Taft-Hartley Act, arbitration will be required under an arbitration clause if the parties cannot be said "with positive assurance" to have excluded the subject from arbitration. *United Steelworkers v. Warrior & Gulf Nav. Co.*, 363 U.S. 574 (1960).

10. **Arbitration Clause** That part of a collective bargaining contract which provides for the use of arbitration as the final step of the grievance procedure. A reference to the Labor Arbitration Rules of the AAA establishes all the procedures necessary for arbitration.

11. **Arbitrator** A person who is given the power to decide a dispute between parties. The labor arbitrator is usually selected because the parties have confidence in his ability to interpret collective bargaining agreements, and have faith in his impartiality. When selected, the arbitrator participates in a system of contractual self-government which the parties themselves have created. The arbitrator is insulated from legal responsibility for his actions. Under AAA administration, the arbitrator acts subject to the provisions of the Voluntary Labor Arbitration Rules.

12. **Arbitrator's Authority** The power of an arbitrator to hear and determine a dispute is derived from law and from the agreement of the parties. The extent of authority can be determined by examining the arbitration agreement.

In *Steelworkers v. Enterprise Wheel & Car Corp.*, Justice Douglas defined the authority of the labor arbitrator as follows: "When an arbitrator is commissioned to interpret and apply the collective bargaining agreement, he is to bring his informed judgment to bear in order to reach a fair solution of a problem. . . . Nevertheless, an arbitrator is confined to interpretation and application of the collective bargaining agreement; he does not sit to dispense his own brand of industrial justice. He may of course look for guidance from many sources, yet his award is legitimate only so long as it draws its essence from the collective bargaining agreement. When the arbitrator's words manifest an infidelity to his obligation, courts have no choice but to refuse enforcement of the award." 363 U.S. 595 (1960)

13. **Award** The decision of an arbitrator in a dispute. The arbitrator's award is based upon the testimony and arguments of both parties. In labor arbitration, the arbitrator's reasons are generally expressed in the form of a written opinion which accompanies the award. The opinion will analyze the evidence and the issues raised by the parties. In a growing number of cases, parties are requesting labor arbitrators to issue a summary award, disposing of the issue but dispensing with much of the editorial material. This procedure can greatly reduce the cost of arbitration.

14. **Award Upon Settlement** An award made at the request of both parties, incorporating terms of a settlement made by parties.

15. **Back Pay Awards** Under most arbitration clauses, an arbitrator may order reinstatement of an employee who has been discharged or suspended without just cause. The arbitrator may reduce the penalty by reinstating the grievant, without back pay, or may reduce back pay to the extent that the employee has been receiving compensation from another job or from unemployment compensation funds. Some contracts restrict the arbitrator's authority to fashion a remedy.

16. **Bias** An arbitrator has a duty to disclose any facts or circumstances that might create a presumption of bias or might disqualify him from serving as an impartial arbitrator. Under Section 17 of the AAA Voluntary Labor Arbitration Rules, such a disclosure is required.

17. **Binding Effect of Arbitration Award** An arbitrator's award is final and binding upon both parties. Labor arbitration awards may be confirmed in court. A judgment entered upon such an award may be enforced in other states. In practice, most labor arbitration awards are accepted as final and binding by the parties; further litigation is rare.

18. **Breach of Contract** To fail to abide by the legal obligations of a contract. A labor grievance is an alleged breach of contract by

the employer. But the union can file a claim under the grievance and arbitration procedure without abandoning its continuing rights under the contract. The United States Supreme Court has stated that "Arbitration provisions, which themselves have not been repudiated, are meant to survive breaches of contract, in many contracts even total breach. . . ." *Drake Bakeries v. Local 50, American Bakery & Confectionery Workers,* 370 U.S. 254 (1962).

19. **Brief** A written statement in support of a party's position, which is submitted to an arbitrator either before or after the hearing. In labor arbitration, briefs are generally used to cite court decisions, prior arbitration awards and the language of the contract. The filing of such briefs tends to prolong the proceeding and to increase the costs of arbitration. Briefs should only be used when they are necessary for the arbitrator's understanding of the case. They are expensive to prepare and time-consuming to read.

20. **Challenge of Arbitrator** A party in arbitration can challenge the impartiality of an arbitrator, with the aim of stopping his appointment or of removing him from office. This right is afforded by Section 17 of the Voluntary Labor Arbitration Rules of the AAA. In practice, such challenges occur very seldom in labor arbitration because the parties know the arbitrators and participate in the selection process.

21. **Closing Argument** A statement customarily made by each party at the close of an arbitration hearing. The arbitrator will always allow the parties to make such a summation if they so desire, but may impose time limitations. Parties frequently use the closing argument to emphasize the points upon which they wish to base their case. Such a presentation leaves their position fresh in the mind of the arbitrator.

22. **Collective Bargaining** Negotiation between an employer and an organization representing a bargaining unit of workers, to create or to make changes in a contract concerning the terms and conditions of employment. Once negotiated and set down in writing, this contract becomes a collective bargaining agreement. In such agreements, the arrangement for settling disputes concerning the interpretation or application of contract provisions is most frequently a grievance and arbitration procedure.

23. **Compensation of the Arbitrator** The fee the arbitrator receives as remuneration for his services. Labor arbitrators in the United States are usually paid on a per diem basis, with reimbursement for travel expenses. The parties generally share such costs equally. When a list is sent to the parties by the AAA, the arbitrator's per diem is disclosed. The arbitrator charges the parties for the entire time he spends on their case. It is possible to reduce the cost of labor arbitration by expediting the hearing procedure, eliminating transcripts and briefs, and by permitting the arbitrator to file a summary award. Under the Expedited Rules of the AAA, labor arbitrators are expected to charge only for the hearing day, substantially reducing the overall cost to the parties.

24. **Compulsory Arbitration** A system under which parties are compelled by law to arbitrate their dispute, sometimes found in statutes relating to bargaining impasses in the public sector. Recent laws in several states have adopted compulsory arbitration for employee groups such as policemen and firemen.

25. **Concurrent Jurisdiction** A situation where one of the parties may be authorized to seek a remedy from the courts, from the National Labor Relations Board or from arbitration. For example, the collective bargaining agreement and the National Labor Relations Act may protect related rights. If a worker is discharged without just cause, his grievance may be subject to arbitration. But if he were discharged for union activities, he may have a right to file an unfair labor practice charge with the NLRB. A question may arise as to which tribunal should have primary jurisdiction. To cope with this conflict, the NLRB has determined, in the *Collyer* case, that the Board will withhold its jurisdiction in favor of arbitration if certain conditions exist. Where an award has been rendered on such a case by an arbitrator, the NLRB may defer to it.

26. **Confirming the Award** A labor arbitrator's award can be converted into a judgment by a court. To complete this process, the winning party must make a motion before the court to have the award confirmed. If all legal requirements have been met, the court will enter judgment. This procedure is seldom necessary in labor arbitration, where parties customarily comply with the requirements set forth in the awards.

27. **Death of an Arbitrator** If a neutral arbitrator dies after being appointed, a successor must be mutually selected by the parties involved or by the administrative agency which appointed him. Section 18 of the Voluntary Labor Arbitration Rules provides for the replacement of an arbitrator.

28. **Default** If a party fails to appear at an arbitration hearing, after due notice, the arbitrator may hear testimony and render an *ex parte* award. Under Section 27 of the AAA Voluntary Labor Arbitration Rules, an award may not be entered solely upon default. The arbitrator must require the party present to submit proof. Such an award can then be enforced in court.

29. **Delegation of the Arbitrator's Authority** The authority of the arbitrator to decide a case cannot be delegated without the consent of both parties. The arbitrator should obtain the written agreement of the parties when he needs to consult outside experts to verify certain facts. The parties have selected the arbitrator for his ability to understand the case and to exercise his judgment. They do not expect him to rely upon the expertise of another.

30. **Delivery of Award** The award is usually mailed to the parties at their last known address by a representative of the AAA or by the arbitrator. If there is no contrary provision in the arbitration clause of the contract or in the applicable rules, the award can be delivered personally or sent by registered or certified mail, or in any other manner prescribed by law.

31. **Demand for Arbitration** The initial notice by one party to the other of an intention to arbitrate under the arbitration clause in their contract. The demand should identify and describe the grievance. It should contain the name of the grievant, the union and the employer, a copy of the arbitration clause, and a statement of the remedy or relief being sought. A copy of the demand should be sent to the opposing party, and another filed with the AAA.

32. **Deposition** The taking of testimony under oath, to be used as evidence in an arbitration. Although arbitrators can order that such depositions be taken, the procedure is seldom necessary in labor arbitration. The testimony is given more weight if it is presented in person by the witness.

33. **Discovery** A procedure invoked before a court trial to inform a party of the facts in a dispute in order to facilitate the attorney's preparation of his case. Discovery is seldom used in labor arbitration, where both parties have participated in an earlier grievance procedure. In rare situations, it may be necessary for adequate preparation. In these cases, discovery procedures are available in arbitration.

34. **Disqualification of Arbitrator** An arbitrator may be disqualified for misconduct. The fact that an arbitrator failed to disclose a personal relationship with the lawyer for one of the parties might constitute sufficient grounds for disqualification. However, if the other party knows of the relationship and fails to object, he may have waived the right to challenge the award.

35. **Duty of Fair Representation** The obligation of a union to safeguard the rights of all members of the bargaining unit. This duty is imposed by Federal labor law. Some union constitutions provide remedies for members who are dissatisfied with the union's handling of their grievances. The union's duty to represent its members in a fair manner does not require that every grievance be carried to arbitration.

36. **Duty to Disclose** The arbitrator must reveal any fact or circumstance related to his ability to render a fair and just award. When notified of his selection, the arbitrator should disclose anything of this nature. If anything develops later which was not previously known, the arbitrator should reveal it at once to the AAA administrator or to the parties.

37. **Enforcement of Arbitration Agreements** Court decisions enforce agreements to arbitrate. The most influential of these decisions was *Textile Workers Union* v. *Lincoln Mills*, where the United States Supreme Court enforced an arbitration clause in a collective bargaining agreement, finding legislative support in Section 301 of the Taft-Hartley Act.

38. **Examination Before Trial** The examination of witnesses before the trial of a case. Most authorities consider this procedure to be incompatible with labor arbitration, where the grievance procedure gives both parties an opportunity to determine the circumstances of the case and to confront witnesses.

39. **Exclusionary Clause** A provision in the collective bargaining agreement which states that specific subjects be excluded from the arbitration process.

40. **Execution of Award** The signing of the award by the arbitrator, with whatever formalities may be required by law. Statutes differ as to their requirements. In some jurisdictions, the signature must be acknowledged. These technical requirements are known to each AAA regional office, so that awards issued in that state can be put in proper form.

41. **Expert Witness** A person with special skill or experience in a profession or with a recognized knowledge of a technical area.

42. **Federal Mediation and Conciliation Service (FMCS)** An independent agency of the Federal Government, established under Title II of the Labor–Management Relations Act, 1947, to mediate and conciliate labor disputes in any industry affecting commerce, other than in the railroad and air transportation industries. One of the major responsibilities imposed on the FMCS by the Labor-Management Relations Act of 1947 is the prevention of labor-management disputes. The FMCS provides governmental facilities for labor contract mediation. The FMCS also maintains a panel of arbitrators, under the jurisdiction of its General Counsel.

43. **Functus Officio** An arbitrator who has completed his task by rendering an award has no further authority. The doctrine of "functus officio," as applied to arbitration, recognizes the termination of an *ad hoc* arbitrator's authority after rendering his award. Under most laws, only the parties or a reviewing court can authorize resubmission to the original arbitrator.

44. **Grievance** A complaint, made on behalf of an employee by his union representative, against an employer, alleging failure to comply with the obligations of the collective bargaining contract. The grievance may result from disciplinary action against the employee. Any complaint relating to employee's pay, working conditions or contract interpretation is generally considered to be a grievance. A grievance may also be a complaint which an employer has against the union.

45. **Grievance Arbitration** The submission of labor grievances to an impartial arbitrator for final determination. Sometimes called arbitration of "rights." Grievances may involve a wide variety of issues. The arbitrator determines the meaning of the contract and clarifies and interprets its terms. Jurisdiction of the arbitrator is sometimes restricted to those disputes which involve the interpretation or application of the contract. Increasingly, arbitrators are required to resolve issues involving the application of various public labor laws, such as unfair labor practices and charges of employment discrimination. Arbitration, in most contracts, is the last step in the grievance procedure.

46. **Grievance Procedure** The steps established in a collective bargaining contract for the handling of complaints made on behalf of employees. A grievance procedure provides a means by which a union or an individual employee can submit a complaint, without disrupting the production process or endangering the employee's job. The primary intent is to settle the dispute as soon as possible.

These procedural steps vary from contract to contract. For example, a grievance may be taken by the shop steward of the aggrieved employee to his supervisor. If no settlement is reached, it may be appealed through successive steps. The grievant may be represented by various union officials. Smaller companies tend to have shorter grievance procedures, consisting of two or three steps. In larger companies, or in multi–plant contracts, there may be grievance committees with union–management representation, followed by joint boards. These systems should be reviewed, from time to time, to assure that they are functioning properly.

47. **Hearing** The presentation of a case in arbitration. The fundamental requirements for a valid hearing are that the arbitrator be present, that the persons whose rights are affected be given notice of the proceedings, and that the parties be heard, and allowed to present all relevant and material evidence and to cross–examine witnesses appearing against them. These rights are fully protected in the Voluntary Labor Arbitration Rules of the AAA.

48. **Impartial Chairman** An arbitrator who is the impartial member of an arbitration board. Such a chairman may be appointed for the duration of the contract, in which case he is

called a permanent chairman. The term is also used to designate the neutral member of an *ad hoc* arbitration board chosen by the mutual consent of the parties. In such a case, the other members of the tribunal may be party-appointed arbitrators, each having been chosen by one of the parties. Usually, it is understood that such persons are partisan.

49. **Impasse** A deadlock in negotiations. When collective bargaining has failed to produce an agreement between the parties, the parties must decide whether to bargain further. Sometimes a strike is called to produce pressure for a settlement.

In some cases, the parties may be willing to use arbitration to help resolve some of the remaining issues. And in public employment, laws are being passed to require that the parties use a variety of settlement techniques, including mediation, fact-finding (with or without the power to make recommendations for settlement), cooling-off periods with various time limits enforceable by court injunction, or final and binding compulsory arbitration.

50. **Individual Rights** Those rights which individual employees still retain despite the designation of a union as their exclusive bargaining agent. An employee may sue his union if he believes it has failed to represent him fairly, but the employee does not usually have an absolute right to have his personal grievance taken to arbitration. Although the union is the representative of all the employees, union interests rest with the majority. The union must be free to decide which grievances should be pursued.

51. **Injunction** A court order restraining a person or an organization from performing an act which would result in serious injury to rights of another person or group. An injunction may require a specific action. Any violation of an injunction is punishable as contempt of court. In rare instances today, injunctions may be used to order a union not to strike. They were more often issued prior to the passage of the Norris-LaGuardia Act in 1932, which limited the powers of federal courts to issue injunctions. A number of states adopted similar statutes. Injunctions may also be used in national emergency disputes under the Taft-Hartley Act, postponing a strike for a period of up to eighty days.

Under the *Boy's Markets* case, courts have been given the power to enjoin wildcat strikes in situations where the union has obligated itself to arbitrate the dispute.

Though injunctive relief is seldom used, some collective agreements give an arbitrator the power to hold an expedited hearing of any claim that the no-strike or no-lockout clause has been violated. If the claim is found to be valid, the arbitrator may enjoin the violation.

52. **Interest Arbitration** The arbitration of the terms of a collective bargaining contract. When contract negotiations reach an impasse and cannot be resolved by collective bargaining, the issues in dispute may be submitted to voluntary arbitration. Several industries have traditionally included provisions for arbitrating new contract terms in their contracts. Even after a strike, the parties may resort to voluntary arbitration. Although unions and employers have been reluctant to accept arbitration as a means of settling interest disputes, in recent years there has been renewed interest in the idea.

53. **Interim Award** Most arbitration statutes in the United States require that arbitration awards be final, and that they determine all of the issues submitted. But where the parties have given expressed or implied consent for an interim award, arbitrators may be authorized to determine some but not all of the issues. Interim awards are sometimes rendered by labor arbitrators in situations where further studies must be made by the parties before the remaining issues can be determined.

54. **Judicial Notice** The recognition by a labor arbitrator of certain facts in a case as being self-evident or of common knowledge. A process whereby arbitrators may recognize statutory laws of other jurisdictions, the official acts of governmental agencies, the common practices in collective bargaining, and all other such matters which are so well-known that a party should not be put to the burden of having to establish them by proof.

55. **Jurisdiction** The legal power or right to exercise authority. The jurisdiction of the labor arbitrator is defined and limited by the agreement of the parties. From time to time, it has been necessary for courts to decide whether the issues in a dispute lie within the

jurisdiction of the arbitrator. But this issue can also be submitted for determination by the arbitrator.

56. **Labor Dispute** A conflict which may include a dispute between parties to a collective bargaining agreement over the terms (interests) or the interpretation of the terms (rights) of their contract. The Norris-LaGuardia Act of March 23, 1932, at § 13(c), defines a labor dispute as follows: "The term 'labor dispute' includes any controversy concerning terms or conditions of employment, or concerning the association or representation of persons in negotiating, fixing, maintaining, changing, or seeking to arrange terms or conditions of employment, regardless of whether or not the disputants stand in the proximate relation of employer and employee."

57. **Laches** Unreasonable delay in asserting a right which might prevent the enforcement of that right. Arbitrators may consider laches when selecting a remedy to a dispute. An arbitrator might rule that a party who has "slept on its claimed rights" for too long has lost its claim to those rights.

58. **Liability of Arbitrator** A labor arbitrator is immune from civil or legal action for any award he may render. Nor is the arbitrator required to explain the reasons for his award, or to testify as to his performance. Without such immunity, a losing party could expose the arbitrator to the hazards of a lawsuit.

59. **Locale of Arbitration** The city where the arbitration is held. In labor arbitration, hearings are generally held at some point that is convenient for the union and the employer, often at the plant or a nearby hotel conference room. Reference to AAA rules in the contract permits the AAA to fix the locale when the parties cannot agree. When an arbitrator is appointed, he will decide where and when the hearing is to be held, in accordance with the mutual convenience and desires of the parties.

60. **Management Rights** Clauses often appear in collective bargaining contracts which reserve management's right to operate the business. Many labor arbitration cases have involved the definition of "management rights." Some contracts go into some detail in specifying these rights. But disputes nevertheless arise as

to whether those rights have been exercised reasonably or whether they have been abandoned by contrary past practice.

61. **Mediation** The participation by a third party in dispute negotiations for the purpose of helping the parties resolve their disagreement. The success of this technique depends on the skill of the mediator. The mediator may meet with the parties separately, or may arrange joint conferences. He tries to facilitate the bargaining process by clarifying the issues and helping the parties to discover areas of possible compromise. The mediator may offer suggestions, but he cannot force either party to accept a solution. Sometimes, the mediator may recommend that the parties agree to arbitrate the remaining issues.

62. **Merging Seniority Lists** The combining of seniority lists when plants or departments within a company consolidate. Various methods for resolving such seniority issues have been developed, involving principles such as length-of-service, follow-the-work, or the surviving-group. Recently, an increasing number of cases have involved mergers intended to eliminate "islands of discrimination."

63. **Merits of a Case** The substantive issues involved in an arbitration case. In its *Trilogy* decisions, the United States Supreme Court ruled that judges are not to consider the merits of the case when they are determining arbitrability or enforcement. Judges should not substitute their judgment for that of the arbitrator.

64. **Modifying the Award** In labor arbitration, the arbitrator's award is the terminal point in the resolution of the grievance. Courts are extremely hesitant to order a rehearing by the arbitrator, or to modify or correct the award. Some arbitration statutes authorize the arbitrator to correct miscalculations of figures or mistakes in the identification of the parties. But in correcting such errors, the arbitrator cannot reexamine the merits of the decision.

65. **Motion to Compel Arbitration** A form of legal action used by the moving party to petition a court to compel the other party to arbitrate. Where a motion to compel is deemed necessary, the supporting affidavits and documents should provide evidence that there is an agreement to arbitrate, that a dispute exists, and that the

opposing party has refused to arbitrate. The court cannot consider the merits of the controversy.

66. **Multiple Grievances** The filing of two or more unrelated grievances by the union, to be heard in a single hearing before the same arbitrator. The union's right to file multiple grievances depends upon contract language and past practice.

67. **National Academy of Arbitrators** An organization founded in 1947, to foster high standards of knowledge and skill on a professional level among those engaged in the arbitration of industrial disputes. The National Academy is not an agency for the selection or appointment of arbitrators. At its annual meeting, lectures on various aspects of arbitration are delivered, which are published by the Bureau of National Affairs under the title, "Proceedings of the Annual Meeting of the National Academy of Arbitrators."

68. **National Labor Relations Board (NLRB)** An independent federal agency created by Congress in 1935 to administer the National Labor Relations Act of July 5, 1935. Under the National Labor Relations Act as amended in 1947 by the Taft-Hartley Act, the NLRB has two primary functions: first, to determine through agency-conducted secret ballot elections which union is to be the exclusive representative of employees for the purpose of collective bargaining; and second, to prevent and remedy unfair labor practices by both labor organizations and employers. Wherever possible, the Board will defer to the parties' existing grievance and arbitration procedures in situations where contractual and unfair labor practice rights are both involved.

69. **National Panel of Labor Arbitrators** A list of some 2,000 persons skilled in labor arbitration, who are available through the twenty-one regional offices of the AAA to serve as arbitrators throughout the United States. Arbitrators are carefully screened by the AAA for impartiality before being appointed to the panel.

70. **No-Strike Clause** A clause in a collective bargaining contract under which the union agrees that it will not strike during the life of the contract. In 1957, the United States Supreme Court held, in *Lincoln Mills*, that an agreement to arbitrate grievances in

a collective bargaining agreement is the "quid pro quo" for a union's promise not to strike.

71. **Notice of Hearing** A formal notification of time and place of a hearing. The rules of the AAA provide that the arbitrator may fix the time and place for each hearing. In doing so, the arbitrator respects the mutual convenience and desires of the parties. Under AAA rules, such a notice must be mailed at least five days in advance.

72. **Open-End Grievance Procedure** A grievance procedure which has as its final step the right to strike. Such agreements are increasingly rare. Most contracts now provide for final and binding arbitration.

73. **Opening Statement** Brief statements made at the opening of a hearing by the advocates, intended to inform the arbitrator of the nature of the dispute and of the evidence they intend to present. It is usual for the claimant to be heard first, but the arbitrator may vary this at his discretion.

74. **Opinion** A written document in which the arbitrator sets forth the reasons for his award. In most labor cases the parties want the arbitrator to explain his reasoning in order to give them some guidance for similar situations that may arise under the contract. But in other situations the parties may ask the AAA to notify the arbitrator that no opinion will be required. This can substantially reduce the cost and delay of arbitration.

75. **Party-Appointed Arbitrator** An arbitrator chosen by one of the parties. It is common for such arbitrators to act in a partisan manner. Party-appointed arbitrators are being used less frequently in labor arbitration, as parties recognize the many ambiguities and problems created by their participation. Most modern grievance arbitration systems provide for a single, neutral arbitrator.

76. **Past Practice** A course of action knowingly followed by a union and a company over a period of time. Where such a pattern exists, the workers involved come to regard it as normal. Past practice becomes significant in arbitration whenever one of the parties submits evidence of it to support its claim. In the *Warrior & Gulf* case, Justice Douglas stated: "The labor arbitrator's source of law is not confined to the express provisions of the contract, as

the industrial common law—the practices of the industry and the shop—is equally a part of the collective bargaining agreement although not expressed in it."

77. **Permanent Arbitrator** An arbitrator who is selected to serve under the terms of a collective bargaining agreement for a specified period of time or for the life of the contract. The duties of the permanent arbitrator are defined in the contract.

78. **Precedent** The concept that prior decisions serve as a rule which must be followed. Prior opinions are not binding upon a labor arbitrator even though they may be considered in determining the case. Prior decisions on the same point may, of course, be treated as precedent by the parties. This is often done in permanent umpire systems. But the general rule in *ad hoc* arbitration is that the arbitrator is not bound by earlier decisions on the same issue. On the other hand, the arbitrator will often find such opinions relevant and analogous to the case under consideration.

79. **Prehearing Conference** A meeting of the arbitrator or an AAA representative with the parties prior to the actual hearing, in order to establish appropriate procedural ground rules or to identify the issues to be determined. Such conferences are seldom necessary in labor arbitration cases. Ordinarily, the grievance procedure has afforded the parties ample opportunity to become familiar with the case and to attempt to settle it. It is customary for arbitrators to encounter the issues, for the first time, at the initial hearing.

80. **Public Employee** A person who is employed by a municipal, county, state, or federal agency. Public employees are subject to various public employment relations laws, which generally have the effect of restricting their freedom to engage in work stoppages, often by replacing the right to strike by various impasse settlement mechanisms.

81. **Recognition Clause** A clause in collective bargaining contracts which commits the employer to dealing with the named union as the bargaining agent for the employees in the unit. Such a commitment is required by the National Labor Relations Act,

which requires an employer to recognize the union that represents a majority of the employees in an appropriate bargaining unit.

82. **Reinstatement** The return of a discharged employee to his former job. The crucial issue in discharge cases is whether the discharge was for just cause and whether the penalty was fair and reasonable. An arbitrator may reinstate an employee with full pay for the time lost, or may reduce such back-pay by various amounts, or may reinstate the employee with no back-pay. Under some contracts, the arbitrator's power to fashion an appropriate remedy has been limited by the parties.

83. **Reopening of Hearings** An arbitrator may reopen a hearing on his own motion or at the request of a party. The arbitrator may wish to reopen the hearings to have the parties clarify the issue or present further testimony. A party may request a rehearing for the presentation of new evidence. Before granting such a request, the arbitrator should offer the opposing party the opportunity to present his objections. If reopening the hearings would delay the award beyond the 30-day time limit specified in the AAA Rules, or beyond the contractual time limits, the matter may not be reopened unless both parties agree.

84. **Residual Rights** The residual rights doctrine gives management the benefit of the doubt concerning rights and powers on which the contract is silent. An arbitrator will examine the contract to determine whether the employer had agreed to reduce the extent of its traditional management rights.

85. **Res Judicata** A legal doctrine to the effect that once an issue has been determined it need not be litigated again. The purpose of the doctrine is to prevent repetitious law suits. Once a case has been properly determined in arbitration, its issues are considered to be *res judicata* as between the parties.

86. **Respondent** In labor arbitration, this term is used for the party against whom the demand for arbitration is asserted. Ordinarily this is the employer.

87. **Right to Counsel** Each party to a labor arbitration has a right to be represented by an advocate. This right is recognized in the AAA Labor Arbitration Rules. There is no requirement that

parties be represented by an attorney. Unions and employers are sometimes represented by lay representatives, persons experienced in labor arbitration.

88. **Rotating Panels** A panel of arbitrators selected on a rotating basis for the life of the contract. By this means, parties to a contract seek to expedite the selection process, while still using arbitrators who are familiar with their contract and relationship. If such rotating panels are administered by the AAA, the arbitrations can be held under its rules.

89. **Rules of Evidence** Courtroom rules of evidence are not applicable in arbitration. Under AAA Labor Arbitration Rules, the arbitrator determines whether evidence is relevant and material. He will determine when hearsay may be admitted, when to accept a copy instead of the original document, and when to admit evidence of oral agreements. Before making a ruling on contested evidence, the arbitrator will listen to the parties' arguments on the issue. Ordinarily, labor arbitrators are willing to accept evidence submitted by either party, for whatever probative value it may have. This attitude should not be abused. An arbitrator is unlikely to be persuaded by irrelevant or immaterial evidence. It is unwise to encroach upon the arbitrator's patience.

90. **Section 301 Disputes** Section 301 of the Taft-Hartley Act reads as follows: "Suits for violation of contracts between an employer and a labor organization representing employees in an industry affecting commerce as defined in this Act, . . . may be brought in any district court of the United States having jurisdiction of the parties, without respect to the amount in controversy or without regard to the citizenship of the parties." In fact, most employers and unions have inserted grievance and arbitration clauses in their contracts in order to eliminate the need for such litigation. The rights created by this Section can be enforced in accordance with the terms of the arbitration clause in the collective bargaining contract.

91. **Seniority** The length of service of an employee in his total employment with that employer, or in some particular seniority unit. Comparative seniority often determines the rights of the employee in relation to other employees, as to layoff, to shift

preference or to promotion. Benefit seniority can affect the individual's rights as to vacation, severance pay or retirement benefits. The seniority rights of an employee are defined in the collective bargaining contract.

92. **Statute of Limitations** A statute which determines the time during which an action may be taken to enforce any legal claim or right. In labor arbitration, the term is also loosely used for the time periods contained in the collective bargaining agreement. These agreements may contain time limitations for performing various acts such as filing a grievance, or appealing the decision of an officer of the company in the grievance procedure. Both courts and arbitrators vary in their treatment of such provisions. The United States Supreme Court in *John Wiley & Sons v. Livingston* held that it is up to the arbitrator to decide whether there was compliance with the time limitations provided in the contract.

93. **Sufficient Ability Clause** A clause in a labor contract creating a standard for determining which employee shall be awarded a particular job. Sufficient ability clauses create minimum acceptable qualifications for doing the work, provided the employee in question has seniority. The interpretation and application of such provisions is a source of many disputes.

94. **Taft-Hartley Act** (Labor Management Relations Act, Pub. L. No. 101, 80th Cong. 1st Sess.; 29 U.S.C.A.§§141–197)

An act, passed in 1947 over President Truman's veto, which modified the National Labor Relations Act by restricting union activities. The Taft-Hartley Law provided special machinery for handling national emergency disputes. It established the Federal Mediation and Conciliation Service. Title 1 of the Taft-Hartley Act has had particular and specific importance for arbitration since the United States Supreme Court based its landmark decision of *Lincoln Mills* on this section, authorizing the enforcement of the arbitration agreement and of the subsequent award.

95. **Transcript of Hearing** A verbatim record of an arbitration hearing, in the form of a stenographic report. The use of a reporter in labor arbitration is the exception rather than the rule. A reporter may be used at the request of either party. If only one party asks for a transcript, that party is obliged to pay for it. Otherwise costs

are shared by both parties. Since the cost of such transcripts can be substantial, parties are able to sharply reduce the costs of arbitration by eliminating the transcript. Labor arbitrators often use tape recorders to refresh their memory as to evidence in extended cases.

96. **Unfair Labor Practice** An act on the part of a union or an employer which interferes with the rights of employees to join labor unions and to engage in collective bargaining. Section 8 of the National Labor Relations Act makes such conduct unlawful and empowers the National Labor Relations Board to prevent or to remedy it. State statutes may also declare certain acts as "unfair labor practices." Arbitrators have no jurisdiction over unfair labor practices except in those cases where such practices also violate collective bargaining agreements.

Court and NLRB Decisions that Have Contributed to the Language of Labor-Management Arbitration:

Lincoln Mills. (1957). The United States Supreme Court ruled that future dispute clauses in collective bargaining agreements in industries affecting interstate commerce can be enforced in Federal Courts under Section 301 (a) of the Taft-Hartley Act. Writing for the majority, Justice William O. Douglas said that the agreement to arbitrate grievance disputes "is the *quid pro quo* for an agreement not to strike." For that reason, he said, Section 301 should be thought of as conferring Federal jurisdiction for the purpose of invoking a remedy for a failure by a party to honor his agreement to arbitrate. Although this decision was narrow in many respects, it formed the basis of establishing the jurisdiction of Federal Courts in labor matters, and led to further important decisions, notably the three often referred to as the *Steelworkers Trilogy*, decided by the U. S. Supreme Court on June 20, 1960.

Warrior & Gulf Navigation Company. By this decision, and by its decision in *American Manufacturing Company* (the second of the three *Steelworkers Trilogy* cases) the court struck down a practice in some lower courts of refusing enforcement of arbitration merely because the grievance seemed to be lacking in merit. It was held that the courts should resolve disputes over arbitrability in favor of coverage unless it could be said "with positive assurance" that the parties excluded the issue from the scope of their arbitration clauses.

Enterprise Wheel & Car Corporation. This was the third decision in the Trilogy. The effect of this ruling was to uphold the arbitrator's authority to remedy violations of collective bargaining agreements. "When an arbitrator is commissioned to interpret and apply the collective bargaining agreement," the court wrote, "he is to bring his informed judgment to bear in order to reach a fair solution of a problem. This is especially true when it comes to formulating remedies. There is a need for flexibility in meeting a wide variety of situations."

Wiley v. *Livingston.* (1964). This U. S. Supreme Court case involved many complicated issues, but centered on whether a collective bargaining agreement survived the purchase of a company by a firm whose employees were not organized. An important part of the decision held that procedural arbitrability (whether time limits and other conditions precedent to arbitration have been complied with) are matters for the arbitrator to determine. This case is distinguishable from *Warrior & Gulf,* where it was held that substantive issues of arbitrability can be determined by the courts.

Spielberg Doctrine. The Taft-Hartley Act forbids discrimination against employees for union activities, and so do virtually all collective bargaining contracts. Thus, when an employee or union accuses an employer of so discriminating, both a contractual and a statutory violation are involved. If a contractual remedy is pursued, does this foreclose the claimant from pursuing his statutory remedy later? In 1955, the NLRB ruled that it would defer to arbitration provided basic safeguards were met. In general, the arbitration had to be fair, and the same issue that would be presented to the NLRB had to have been considered by the arbitrator. Courts have upheld the Board's right to decline jurisdiction of "dual jurisdiction" cases under such circumstances.

In *Collyer,* (1971), the NLRB withheld jurisdiction, when the issues involved could be determined under an arbitration clause, subject to the matter being brought back for further review after being determined in the grievance procedure or pursuant to an arbitrator's award.

Under *Alexander v. Gardner-Denver,* (1974), Title VII rights of the individual employee are handled differently. The U.S. Supreme Court held that an employee's right to a trial *de novo* of a claim of race or sex discrimination is not foreclosed by an unfavorable arbitration award under the nondiscrimination clause, but the trial judge should give "great weight" to the arbitrator's decision.

Boy's Markets, Inc. (1970). The essence of the holding of the U.S. Supreme Court is that an award enjoining a strike in violation of a collective bargaining agreement is enforceable, notwithstanding the Norris-LaGuardia Act's proscription of injunctions in labor disputes.

A Selected Bibliography of Books on Labor Arbitration, Including Arbitration by Public Employees

Aaron, Benjamin and others. *The Future of Labor Arbitration in America.* New York, American Arbitration Association, 1976.

Abersold, John R. and Wayne E. Howard. *Cases in Labor Relations: An Arbitration Process.* Englewood Cliffs, N.J.: Prentice-Hall, 1967.

American Arbitration Association. Education Department. *Arbitration of Police and Fire Fighter Disputes.* New York: 1971.

American Assembly. *Public Workers and Public Unions.* Englewood Cliffs, N.J.: Prentice-Hall, 1972.

American Association of Industrial Management. *Grievance Procedures; Arbitration.* Philadelphia: 1969.

Anderson, Howard J., ed. *The Role of the Neutral in Public Employee Disputes; A Report of the Joint Conference of the Association of Labor Mediation Agencies and the National Association of State Labor Relations Agencies, June 21 to June 25, 1971.* Washington: Bureau of National Affairs, 1972.

Baderschneider, Earl R. and Paul F. Miller, eds. *Labor Arbitration in Health Care. A Case Book.* New York: Spectrum Publications, Inc., 1976.

Baer, Walter E. *Discipline and Discharge Under the Labor Agreement.* New York: American Management Association, 1972.

______. *Grievance Handling: 101 Guides for Supervisors.* New York: American Arbitration Association, 1970.

______. *Practice and Precedent in Labor Relations.* Lexington, Mass.: Lexington Books, 1972.

Beatty, Marion. *Labor-Management Arbitration Manual*. New York: E.E. Eppler, 1960.

Bernstein, Merton C. *Private Dispute Settlement*. New York: Free Press, 1968.

Blackman, John L., Jr. *Presidential Seizure in Labor Disputes*. Cambridge, Mass.: Harvard University Press, 1967.

Carlton, Patrick W. and Harold I. Goodwin. *The Collective Dilemma: Negotiations in Education*. Worthington, Ohio: Charles A. Jones, 1969.

Chamberlain, Neil W. and James W. Kuhn. *Collective Bargaining*. 2d ed. New York: McGraw-Hill, 1965.

Clark, R. Theodore, Jr. *Compulsory Arbitration in Public Employment*. Chicago: Public Personnel Association, 1972.

Cole, David L. *The Quest for Industrial Peace*. New York: McGraw-Hill, 1963.

Connery, Robert H. and William V. Farr, eds. *Unionization of Municipal Employees; Proceedings of the Academy of Political Science*. New York: Academy of Political Science, Columbia, 1970.

Cox, Archibald and Derek Curtis Bok. *Cases and Materials on Labor Law*. 6th ed. Brooklyn: Foundation Press, 1965.

Davey, Harold W. *Arbitration as a Substitute for Other Legal Remedies*. Ames: Industrial Relations Center, Iowa State University, 1972.

———. *Contemporary Collective Bargaining*. 3d ed. Englewood Cliffs, N.J.: Prentice-Hall, 1972.

Dunlop, John T. and Neil W. Chamberlain, eds. *Frontiers of Collective Bargaining*. New York: Harper and Row, 1967.

Eggert, Gerald G. *Railroad Labor Disputes; The Beginning of Federal Strike Policy*. Ann Arbor, Mich.: University of Michigan Press, 1967.

Elam, Stanley, Myron Lieberman and Michael H. Moskow. *Readings on Collective Negotiations in Public Education.* Chicago: Rand McNally, 1967.

Elkouri, Frank and Edna Asper Elkouri. *How Arbitration Works.* Rev. ed. Washington: Bureau of National Affairs, 1960.

Fleming, Robben Wright. *The Labor Arbitration Process.* Urbana, Ill.: University of Illinois Press, 1965.

Gilroy, Thomas P., ed. *Dispute Settlement in the Public Sector.* Iowa City: Center for Labor and Management, University of Iowa, 1972.

Gilroy, Thomas P. and Anthony V. Sinicropi. *Collective Negotiations and Public Administration.* Iowa City: Center for Labor and Management, College of Business Administration, University of Iowa, 1970.

______. *Dispute Settlement in the Public Sector: The State-of-the-Art, Report Submitted to Division of Public Employee Labor Relations, Office of Labor Management Relations Services, United States Department of Labor.* Washington: Government Printing Office, 1972.

Gilroy, Thomas P., Anthony V. Sinicropi, Franklin D. Stone and Theodore R. Urich. *Educator's Guide to Collective Negotiations.* Columbus, Ohio: Charles E. Merrill, 1969.

Government Employee Relations Report. no. 1– 1963– Washington: Bureau of National Affairs.

Greenman, Russell L. and Eric J. Schmertz. *Personnel Administration and the Law.* Washington: Bureau of National Affairs, 1972.

Gregory, Charles Oscar. *Labor and the Law.* 2d rev. ed., with 1961 supplement. New York: Norton, 1961.

Grievance Guide for Unions; Arbitration Awards from BNA's Union Labor Report. 3d ed. Washington: Bureau of National Affairs, 1968.

Hays, Paul R. *Labor Arbitration; A Dissenting View.* New Haven: Yale University Press, 1966.

Horton, Raymond D. *Municipal Labor Relations in New York City: Lessons of the Lindsay-Wagner Years.* New York: Praeger, 1973.

Institute of Collective Bargaining and Group Relations. *Collective Bargaining Today; Proceedings of the Collective Bargaining Forum—1969.* Washington: Bureau of National Affairs, 1970.

———. *Collective Bargaining Today; Proceedings of the Collective Bargaining Forum—1970.* Washington: Bureau of National Affairs, 1971.

Jones, Dallas L. *Arbitration and Industrial Discipline.* Ann Arbor, Mich.: Bureau of Industrial Relations, University of Michigan, 1961.

Kagel, Sam. *Anatomy of a Labor Arbitration.* Washington: Bureau of National Affairs, 1961.

Keller, Leonard A. *The Management Function: A Positive Approach to Labor Relations.* Washington: Bureau of National Affairs, 1963.

Kruger, Daniel H. and Charles T. Schmidt, Jr., eds. *Collective Bargaining in the Public Service.* New York: Random House, 1969.

Lieberman, Myron and Michael H. Moskow. *Collective Negotiations for Teachers; An Approach to School Administration.* Chicago: Rand McNally, 1966.

Loewenberg, J. Joseph and Michael H. Moskow, eds. *Collective Bargaining in Government; Readings and Cases.* Englewood Cliffs, N.J.: Prentice-Hall, 1972.

Maggiola, Walter A. *Techniques of Mediation in Labor Disputes.* Dobbs Ferry, N.Y.: Oceana, 1971.

Marx, Herbert L., Jr., ed. *Collective Bargaining for Public Employees.* New York: Wilson, 1969.

Meltzer, Bernard D. *Appendix to Labor Law; Cases, Materials and Problems.* Boston: Little, Brown, 1970.

______. *Labor Law; Cases, Materials and Problems*. Boston: Little Brown, 1970.

Metzger, Norman and Dennis D. Pointer. *Labor-Management Relations in the Health Services Industry: Theory and Practice*. Washington: Science and Health Publications, 1972.

Moskow, Michael H. *Teachers and Unions*. Philadelphia: University of Pennsylvania, Wharton School of Finance and Commerce, Industrial Research Unit, 1966.

Moskow, Michael H., J. Joseph Loewenberg and Edward Clifford Koziara. *Collective Bargaining in Public Employment*. New York: Random House, 1970.

Murphy, Richard J. and Morris Sackman, eds. *The Crisis in Public Employee Relations in the Decade of the Seventies; Proceedings of a Seminar* . . . Washington: Bureau of National Affairs, 1970.

National Academy of Arbitrators. *Proceedings of the Annual Meeting*. 1st–7th– 1948–54– Washington: Bureau of National Affairs.

New York University. *Proceedings of the Annual Conference on Labor*. 1st– 1948– New York: Matthew Bender.

Northrup, Herbert R. *Compulsory Arbitration and Government Intervention in Labor Disputes; An Analysis of Experience*. Washington: Labor Policy Association, 1966.

Power, Luke, ed. *Seminar on Collective Bargaining: 1966* . . . St. Bonaventure, N.Y.: St. Bonaventure University Press, 1967.

______, ed. *Seminar on Collective Bargaining: 1967* . . . Jamestown, N.Y.: Jamestown Community College Press, 1968.

______, ed. *Seminar on Collective Bargaining: 1972* . . . Niagara Falls, N.Y.: Niagara University Press, 1972.

Prasow, Paul and Edward Peters. *Arbitration and Collective Bargaining: Conflict Resolution in Labor Relations.* New York: McGraw-Hill, 1970.

Roberts, Harold S., ed. *Compulsory Arbitration: Panacea or Millstone?* Honolulu: Industrial Relations Center, University of Hawaii, 1965.

———. *Labor-Management Relations in the Public Service.* 5th ed. Honolulu: University of Hawaii Press, 1970.

———. *A Manual for Employee-Management Cooperation in the Federal Service.* 3d ed. Honolulu: Industrial Relations Center, University of Hawaii, 1967.

———. *Roberts' Dictionary of Industrial Relations.* Rev. ed. Washington: Bureau of National Affairs, 1971.

Seide, Katharine, ed. *A Dictionary of Arbitration and its Terms.* Dobbs Ferry, N.Y.: Oceana, 1970.

Sherman, Herbert L., Jr. *Arbitration of the Steel Wage Structure; Guides, Principles and Framework for the Settlement of Job Description and Classification Disputes and Related Problems.* Pittsburgh: University of Pittsburgh Press, 1961.

Shils, Edward B. and C. Taylor Whittier. *Teachers, Administrators and Collective Bargaining.* New York: Thomas Y. Crowell, 1968.

Simkin, William E. *Mediation and the Dynamics of Collective Bargaining.* Washington: Bureau of National Affairs, 1971.

Slichter, Sumner H., James J. Healy and E. Robert Livernash. *The Impact of Collective Bargaining on Management.* Washington: Brookings Institution, 1960.

Slovenko, Ralph, ed. *Symposium on Labor Relations Law.* Baton Rouge, La.: Claitor's Bookstore, 1961.

Smith, Russell A., Leroy S. Merrifield and Donald P. Rothschild. *Collective Bargaining and Labor Arbitration; Materials on the Negotiation, Enforcement and Content of the Labor Agreement.* Indianapolis: Bobbs-Merrill, 1970.

Southwestern Legal Foundation. *Labor Law Developments; Proceedings of . . . [the] Annual Institute on Labor Law.* 1st– 1954– Washington: Bureau of National Affairs, 1955– Matthew Bender publisher beginning with the 1968 proceedings.

Staudohar, Paul D. *Public Employment Disputes and Dispute Settlement.* Honolulu: Industrial Relations Center, University of Hawaii, 1972.

Stone, Morris. *Labor Grievances and Decisions.* New York: American Arbitration Association, 1970.

______. *Labor-Management Contracts at Work; Analysis of Awards Reported by the American Arbitration Association.* New York: Harper and Row, 1961.

______. *Managerial Freedom and Job Security.* New York: Harper and Row, 1964.

Summers, Clyde W. and Harry H. Wellington. *Cases and Materials on Labor Law.* Mineola, N.Y.: Foundation Press, 1968.

Tice, Terrence N., ed. *Faculty Power: Collective Bargaining on Campus.* Ann Arbor, Mich.: The Institute of Continuing Legal Education, 1972.

Tracy, Estelle R., ed. *Arbitration Cases in Public Employment.* New York: American Arbitration Association, 1969.

Trotta, Maurice S. *Labor Arbitration; Principles, Practices, Issues.* New York: Simons-Boardman, 1961.

Trotta, Maurice S. and Walter W. Bishop. *Grievance Handling for Foremen.* Ann Arbor, Mich.: Bureau of Industrial Relations, Graduate School of Business Administration, University of Michigan, 1969.

United States Bureau of Labor Statistics. *Major Collective Bargaining Agreements; Arbitration Procedures.* Washington: Government Printing Office, 1970.

Updegraff, Clarence M. *Arbitration and Labor Relations.* 3d ed. Washington: Bureau of National Affairs, 1970.

Vosloo, Willem B. *Collective Bargaining in the United States Federal Civil Service.* Chicago: Public Personnel Association, 1966.

Walsh, R., ed. *Sorry . . . No Government Today; Unions vs. City Hall.* Boston: Beacon Press, 1969.

Warner, Kenneth O., ed. *Collective Bargaining in the Public Service: Theory and Practice.* Chicago: Public Personnel Association, 1967.

Wellington, Harry H. and Ralph K. Winters, Jr. *The Unions and the Cities.* Washington: Brookings Institute, 1971.

Werne, Benjamin, ed. *Current Labor-Management Problems.* New York: Practising Law Institute, 1969.

Wiggins, Ronald L. *The Arbitration of Industrial Engineering Disputes.* Washington: Bureau of National Affairs, 1970.

Wolfbein, Semour L., ed. *Emerging Sectors of Collective Bargaining.* Braintree, Mass.: D.H. Mark, 1970.

Wollet, Donald H. and Don W. Sears. *Collective Bargaining in Public Employment.* Washington: Bureau of National Affairs, 1971.

Woodworth, Robert T. and Richards B. Peterson. *Collective Negotiations for Public and Professional Employees; Text and Readings.* Glenview, Ill.: Scott, Foresman, 1969.

Wortman, Max S. and George C. Witteried. *Labor Relations and Collective Bargaining; Text and Cases.* Boston: Allyn and Bacon, 1969.

Yaffe, Byron and Howard Goldblatt. *Factfinding in Public Employment Disputes in New York State: More Promise than Illusion.* Ithaca, N.Y.: New York State School of Industrial and Labor Relations, 1971.

Classification Guide

This is a listing of all main heads currently used in the index to **Summary of Labor Arbitration Awards.**

American Arbitration Association Voluntary Labor Arbitration Rules

1. **Agreement of Parties**—The parties shall be deemed to have made these Rules a part of their arbitration agreement whenever, in a collective bargaining agreement or submission, they have provided for arbitration by the American Arbitration Association (hereinafter AAA) or under its Rules. These Rules shall apply in the form obtaining at the time the arbitration is initiated.

2. **Name of Tribunal**—Any Tribunal constituted by the parties under these Rules shall be called the Voluntary Labor Arbitration Tribunal.

3. **Administrator**—When parties agree to arbitrate under these Rules and an arbitration is instituted thereunder, they thereby authorize the AAA to administer the arbitration. The authority and obligations of the Administrator are as provided in the agreement of the parties and in these Rules.

4. **Delegation of Duties**—The duties of the AAA may be carried out through such representatives or committees as the AAA may direct.

5. **National Panel of Labor Arbitrators**—The AAA shall establish and maintain a National Panel of Labor Arbitrators and shall appoint arbitrators therefrom, as hereinafter provided.

6. **Office of Tribunal**—The general office of the Labor Arbitration Tribunal is the headquarters of the AAA, which may, however, assign the administration of an arbitration to any of its Regional Offices.

7. **Initiation Under an Arbitration Clause in a Collective Bargaining Agreement**—Arbitration under an arbitration clause in a collective bargaining agreement under these Rules may be initiated by either party in the following manner:

(a) By giving written notice to the other party of intention to arbitrate (Demand), which notice shall contain a statement setting forth the nature of the dispute and the remedy sought, and

(b) By filing at any Regional Office of the AAA three copies of said notice, together with a copy of the collective bargaining agreement, or such parts thereof as relate to the dispute, including the arbitration provisions. After the Arbitrator is appointed, no new or different claim may be submitted to him except with the consent of the Arbitrator and all other parties.

8. **Answer**—The party upon whom the demand for arbitration is made may file an answering statement with the AAA within seven days after notice from the AAA, in which event he shall simultaneously send a copy of his answer to the other party. If no answer is filed within the stated time, it will be assumed that the claim is denied. Failure to file an answer shall not operate to delay the arbitration.

9. **Initiation under a Submission**—Parties to any collective bargaining agreement may initiate an arbitration under these Rules by filing at any Regional Office of the AAA two copies of a written agreement to arbitrate under these Rules (Submission), signed by the parties and setting forth the nature of the dispute and the remedy sought.

10. **Fixing of Locale**—The parties may mutually agree upon the locale where the arbitration is to be held. If the locale is not designated in the collective bargaining agreement or submission, and if there is a dispute as to the appropriate locale, the AAA shall have the power to determine the locale and its decision shall be binding.

11. **Qualifications of Arbitrator**—No person shall serve as a neutral Arbitrator in any arbitration in which he has any financial

or personal interest in the result of the arbitration, unless the parties, in writing, waive such disqualification.

12. **Appointment from Panel**—If the parties have not appointed an Arbitrator and have not provided any other method of appointment, the Arbitrator shall be appointed in the following manner: Immediately after the filing of the Demand or Submission, the AAA shall submit simultaneously to each party an identical list of names of persons chosen from the Labor Panel. Each party shall have seven days from the mailing date in which to cross off any names to which he objects, number the remaining names indicating the order of his preference, and return the list to the AAA. If a party does not return the list within the time specified, all persons named therein shall be deemed acceptable. From among the persons who have been approved on both lists, and in accordance with the designated order of mutual preference, the AAA shall invite the acceptance of an Arbitrator to serve. If the parties fail to agree upon any of the persons named or if those named decline or are unable to act, or if for any other reason the appointment cannot be made from the submitted lists, the Administrator shall have power to make the appointment from other members of the Panel without the submission of any additional lists.

13. **Direct Appointment by Parties**—If the agreement of the parties names an Arbitrator or specifies a method of appointing an Arbitrator, that designation or method shall be followed. The notice of appointment, with the name and address of such Arbitrator, shall be filed with the AAA by the appointing party.

If the agreement specifies a period of time within which an Arbitrator shall be appointed, and any party fails to make such appointment within that period, the AAA may make the appointment.

If no period of time is specified in the agreement, the AAA shall notify the parties to make the appointment and if within seven days thereafter such Arbitrator has not been so appointed, the AAA shall make the appointment.

14. **Appointment of Neutral Arbitrator by Party-Appointed Arbitrators**—If the parties have appointed their Arbitrators, or if either or both of them have been appointed as provided in Section 13, and have authorized such Arbitrators to appoint a neutral

Arbitrator within a specified time and no appointment is made within such time or any agreed extension thereof, the AAA may appoint a neutral Arbitrator, who shall act as Chairman.

If no period of time is specified for appointment of the neutral Arbitrator and the parties do not make the appointment within seven days from the date of the appointment of the last party-appointed Arbitrator, the AAA shall appoint such neutral Arbitrator, who shall act as Chairman.

If the parties have agreed that the Arbitrators shall appoint the neutral Arbitrator from the Panel, the AAA shall furnish to the party-appointed Arbitrators, in the manner prescribed in Section 12, a list selected from the Panel, and the appointment of the neutral Arbitrator shall be made as prescribed in such Section.

15. **Number of Arbitrators**—If the arbitration agreement does not specify the number of Arbitrators, the dispute shall be heard and determined by one Arbitrator, unless the parties otherwise agree.

16. **Notice to Arbitrator of His Appointment**—Notice of the appointment of the neutral Arbitrator shall be mailed to the Arbitrator by the AAA and the signed acceptance of the Arbitrator shall be filed with the AAA prior to the opening of the first hearing.

17. **Disclosure by Arbitrator of Disqualification**—Prior to accepting his appointment, the prospective neutral Arbitrator shall disclose any circumstances likely to create a presumption of bias or which he believes might disqualify him as an impartial Arbitrator. Upon receipt of such information, the AAA shall immediately disclose it to the parties. If either party declines to waive the presumptive disqualification, the vacancy thus created shall be filled in accordance with the applicable provisions of these Rules.

18. **Vacancies**—If any Arbitrator should resign, die, withdraw, refuse or be unable or disqualified to perform the duties of his office, the AAA shall, on proof satisfactory to it, declare the office vacant. Vacancies shall be filled in the same manner as that governing the making of the original appointment, and the matter shall be reheard by the new Arbitrator.

19. **Time and Place of Hearing**—The Arbitrator shall fix the time and place for each hearing. At least five days prior thereto the AAA shall mail notice of the time and place of hearing to each party, unless the parties otherwise agree.

20. **Representation by Counsel**—Any party may be represented at the hearing by counsel or by other Authorized representative.

21. **Stenographic Record**—Any party may request a stenographic record by making arrangements for same through the AAA. If such transcript is agreed by the parties to be, or in appropriate cases determined by the arbitrator to be the official record of the proceeding, it must be made available to the arbitrator, and to the other party for inspection, at a time and place determined by the arbitrator. The total cost of such a record shall be shared equally by those parties that order copies.

22. **Attendance at Hearings**—Persons having a direct interest in the arbitration are entitled to attend hearings. The Arbitrator shall have the power to require the retirement of any witness or witnesses during the testimony of other witnesses. It shall be discretionary with the Arbitrator to determine the propriety of the attendance of any other persons.

23. **Adjournments**—The Arbitrator for good cause shown may adjourn the hearing upon the request of a party or upon his own initiative, and shall adjourn when all the parties agree thereto.

24. **Oaths**—Before proceeding with the first hearing, each Arbitrator may take an Oath of Office, and if required by law, shall do so. The Arbitrator may, in his discretion, require witnesses to testify under oath administered by any duly qualified person, and if required by law or requested by either party, shall do so.

25. **Majority Decision**—Whenever there is more than one Arbitrator, all decisions of the Arbitrators shall be by majority vote. The award shall also be made by majority vote unless the concurrence of all is expressly required.

26. **Order of Proceedings**—A hearing shall be opened by the filing of the oath of the Arbitrator, where required, and by the recording of the place, time and date of hearing, the presence of

the Arbitrator and parties, and counsel if any, and the receipt by the Arbitrator of the Demand and Answer, if any, or the Submission.

Exhibits, when offered by either party, may be received in evidence by the Arbitrator. The names and addresses of all witnesses and exhibits in order received shall be made a part of the record.

The Arbitrator may, in his discretion, vary the normal procedure under which the initiating party first presents his claim, but in any case shall afford full and equal opportunity to all parties for presentation of relevant proofs.

27. **Arbitration in the Absence of a Party**—Unless the law provides to the contrary, the arbitration may proceed in the absence of any party, who, after due notice, fails to be present or fails to obtain an adjournment. An award shall not be made solely on the default of a party. The Arbitrator shall require the other party to submit such evidence as he may require for the making of an award.

28. **Evidence**—The parties may offer such evidence as they desire and shall produce such additional evidence as the Arbitrator may deem necessary to an understanding and determination of the dispute. When the Arbitrator is authorized by law to subpoena witnesses and documents, he may do so upon his own initiative or upon the request of any party. The Arbitrator shall be the judge of the relevancy and materiality of the evidence offered and conformity to legal rules of evidence shall not be necessary. All evidence shall be taken in the presence of all of the Arbitrators and all of the parties except where any of the parties is absent in default or has waived his right to be present.

29. **Evidence by Affidavit and Filing of Documents**—The Arbitrator may receive and consider the evidence of witnesses by affidavit, but shall give it only such weight as he deems proper after consideration of any objections made to its admission.

All documents not filed with the Arbitrator at the hearing but which are arranged at the hearing or subsequently by agreement of the parties to be submitted, shall be filed with the AAA for transmission to the Arbitrator. All parties shall be afforded opportunity to examine such documents.

30. **Inspection**—Whenever the Arbitrator deems it necessary, he may make an inspection in connection with the subject matter of the dispute after written notice to the parties who may, if they so desire, be present at such inspection.

31. **Closing of Hearings**—The Arbitrator shall inquire of all parties whether they have any further proofs to offer or witnesses to be heard. Upon receiving negative replies, the Arbitrator shall declare the hearings closed and a minute thereof shall be recorded. If briefs or other documents are to be filed, the hearings shall be declared closed as of the final date set by the Arbitrator for filing with the AAA. The time limit within which the Arbitrator is required to make his award shall commence to run, in the absence of other agreement by the parties, upon the closing of the hearings.

32. **Reopening of Hearings**—The hearings may be reopened by the Arbitrator on his own motion, or on the motion of either party, for good cause shown, at any time before the award is made, but if the reopening of the hearing would prevent the making of the award within the specific time agreed upon by the parties in the contract out of which the controversy has arisen, the matter may not be reopened, unless both parties agree upon the extension of such time limit. When no specific date is fixed in the contract, the Arbitrator may reopen the hearings, and the Arbitrator shall have 30 days from the closing of the reopened hearings within which to make an award.

33. **Waiver of Rules**—Any party who proceeds with the arbitration after knowledge that any provision or requirement of these Rules has not been complied with and who fails to state his objection thereto in writing, shall be deemed to have waived his right to object.

34. **Waiver of Oral Hearing**—The parties may provide, by written agreement, for the waiver of oral hearings. If the parties are unable to agree as to the procedure, the AAA shall specify a fair and equitable procedure.

35. **Extensions of Time**—The parties may modify any period of time by mutual agreement. The AAA for good cause may extend any period of time established by these Rules, except the time for

making the award. The AAA shall notify the parties of any such extension of time and its reason therefor.

36. **Serving of Notices**—Each party to a Submission or other agreement which provides for arbitration under these Rules shall be deemed to have consented and shall consent that any papers, notices or process necessary or proper for the initiation or continuation of an arbitration under these Rules and for any court action in connection therewith or the entry of judgment on an award made thereunder, may be served upon such party (a) by mail addressed to such party or his attorney at his last known address, or (b) by personal service, within or without the state wherein the arbitration is to be held.

37. **Time of Award**—The award shall be rendered promptly by the Arbitrator and, unless otherwise agreed by the parties, or specified by the law, not later than thirty days from the date of closing the hearings, or if oral hearings have been waived, then from the date of transmitting the final statements and proofs to the Arbitrator.

38. **Form of Award**—The award shall be in writing and shall be signed either by the neutral Arbitrator or by a concurring majority if there be more than one Arbitrator. The parties shall advise the AAA whenever they do not require the Arbitrator to accompany the award with an opinion.

39. **Award Upon Settlement**—If the parties settle their dispute during the course of the arbitration, the Arbitrator, upon their request, may set forth the terms of the agreed settlement in an award.

40. **Delivery of Award to Parties**—Parties shall accept as legal delivery of the award the placing of the award or a true copy thereof in the mail by the AAA, addressed to such party at his last known address or to his attorney, or personal service of the award, or the filing of the award in any manner which may be prescribed by law.

41. **Release of Documents for Judicial Proceedings**—The AAA shall, upon the written request of a party, furnish to such party at

his expense certified facsimiles of any papers in the AAA's possession that may be required in judicial proceedings relating to the arbitration.

42. **Judicial Proceedings**—The AAA is not a necessary party in judicial proceedings relating to the arbitration.

43. **Administrative Fee**—As a nonprofit organization, the AAA shall prescribe an administrative fee schedule to compensate it for the cost of providing administrative services. The schedule in effect at the time of filing shall be applicable.

44. **Expenses**—The expenses of witnesses for either side shall be paid by the party producing such witnesses.

Expenses of the arbitration, other than the cost of the stenographic record, including required traveling and other expenses of the Arbitrator and of AAA representatives, and the expenses of any witnesses or the cost of any proofs produced at the direct request of the Arbitrator, shall be borne equally by the parties unless they agree otherwise, or unless the Arbitrator in his award assesses such expenses or any part thereof against any specified party or parties.

45. **Communication with Arbitrator**—There shall be no communication between the parties and a neutral Arbitrator other than at oral hearings. Any other oral or written communications from the parties to the Arbitrator shall be directed to the AAA for transmittal to the Arbitrator.

46. **Interpretation and Application of Rules**—The Arbitrator shall interpret and apply these Rules insofar as they relate to his powers and duties. When there is more than one Arbitrator and a difference arises among them concerning the meaning or application of any such Rules, it shall be decided by majority vote. If that is unobtainable, either Arbitrator or party may refer the question to the AAA for final decision. All other Rules shall be interpreted and applied by the AAA.

Expedited Labor Arbitration

Recently there has been increasing concern over rising costs and delays in grievance arbitration. The Labor-Management Committee of the American Arbitration Association recommended the establishment of an expedited procedure, under which cases could be scheduled promptly and an award rendered within five days of the hearing. Simplified procedures would also reduce the cost.

In return for giving up their right to some of the procedural advantages of traditional labor arbitration, the parties could get a quick decision, at a reduced cost.

These Expedited Rules provide such a procedure for use in appropriate cases. Many of the leading labor arbitrators have indicated a willingness to offer their services. Now, it is up to the labor-management community to use this system to its maximum benefit.

American Arbitration Association Expedited Labor Arbitration Rules

1. **Agreement of Parties**—These Rules shall apply whenever the parties have agreed to arbitrate under them, in the form obtaining at the time the arbitration is initiated.

2. **Appointment of Neutral Arbitrator**—The AAA shall appoint a single neutral Arbitrator from its Panel of Labor Arbitrators, who shall hear and determine the case promptly.

3. **Initiation of Expedited Arbitration Proceeding**—Cases may be initiated by joint submission in writing, or in accordance with a collective bargaining agreement.

4. **Qualifications of Neutral Arbitrator**—No person shall serve as a neutral Arbitrator in any arbitration in which that person has any financial or personal interest in the result of the arbitration. Prior to accepting an appointment, the prospective Arbitrator shall disclose any circumstances likely to prevent a prompt hearing or to create a presumption of bias. Upon receipt of such information, the AAA shall immediately replace that Arbitrator or communicate the information to the parties.

5. **Vacancy**—The AAA is authorized to substitute another Arbitrator if a vacancy occurs or if an appointed Arbitrator is unable to serve promptly.

6. **Time and Place of Hearing**—The AAA shall fix a mutually convenient time and place of the hearing, notice of which must be given at least 24 hours in advance. Such notice may be given orally.

7. **Representation by Counsel**—Any party may be represented at the hearing by counsel or other representative.

8. **Attendance at Hearings**—Persons having a direct interest in the arbitration are entitled to attend hearings. The Arbitrator may require the retirement of any witness during the testimony of other witnesses. The Arbitrator shall determine whether any other person may attend the hearing.

9. **Adjournments**—Hearings shall be adjourned by the Arbitrator only for good cause, and an appropriate fee will be charged by the AAA against the party causing the adjournment.

10. **Oaths**—Before proceeding with the first hearing, the Arbitrator shall take an oath of office. The Arbitrator may require witnesses to testify under oath.

11. **No Stenographic Record**—There shall be no stenographic record of the proceedings.

12. **Proceedings**—The hearing shall be conducted by the Arbitrator in whatever manner will most expeditiously permit full presentation of the evidence and the arguments of the parties. The Arbitrator shall make an appropriate minute of the proceedings. Normally, the hearing shall be completed within one day. In unusual circumstances and for good cause shown, the Arbitrator may schedule an additional hearing, within five days.

13. **Arbitration in the Absence of a Party**—The arbitration may proceed in the absence of any party who, after due notice, fails to be present. An award shall not be made solely on the default of a party. The Arbitrator shall require the attending party to submit supporting evidence.

14. **Evidence**—The Arbitrator shall be the sole judge of the relevancy and materiality of the evidence offered.

15. **Evidence by Affidavit and Filing of Documents**—The Arbitrator may receive and consider evidence in the form of an affidavit, but shall give appropriate weight to any objections made. All documents to be considered by the Arbitrator shall be filed at the hearing. There shall be no post hearing briefs.

16. **Close of Hearings**—The Arbitrator shall ask whether parties have any further proofs to offer or witnesses to be heard. Upon receiving negative replies, the Arbitrator shall declare and note the hearing closed.

17. **Waiver of Rules**—Any party who proceeds with the arbitration after knowledge that any provision or requirement of these Rules has not been complied with and who fails to state his objections thereto in writing shall be deemed to have waived his right to object.

18. **Serving of Notices**—Any papers or process necessary or proper for the initiation or continuation of an arbitration under these Rules and for any court action in connection therewith or for the entry of judgment on an Award made thereunder, may be served upon such party (a) by mail addressed to such party or its

attorney at its last known address, or (b) by personal service, or (c) as otherwise provided in these Rules.

19. **Time of Award**—The award shall be rendered promptly by the Arbitrator and, unless otherwise agreed by the parties, not later than five business days from the date of the closing of the hearing.

20. **Form of Award**—The Award shall be in writing and shall be signed by the Arbitrator. If the Arbitrator determines that an opinion is necessary, it shall be in summary form.

21. **Delivery of Award to Parties**—Parties shall accept as legal delivery of the award the placing of the award or a true copy thereof in the mail by the AAA, addressed to such party at its last known address or to its attorney, or personal service of the award, or the filing of the award in any manner which may be prescribed by law.

22. **Expenses**—The expenses of witnesses for either side shall be paid by the party producing such witnesses.

23. **Interpretation and Application of Rules**—The Arbitrator shall interpret and apply these Rules insofar as they relate to his powers and duties. All other Rules shall be interpreted and applied by the AAA, as Administrator.

THE AAA HAS MADE SPECIAL ARRANGEMENTS TO REDUCE THE COST OF ARBITRATION UNDER THESE RULES. DETAILS ARE AVAILABLE AT THE AAA REGIONAL OFFICE ADMINISTERING THE CASE.

The United States Arbitration Act

Title 9, U.S. Code §§1–14, first enacted February 12, 1925 (43 Stat. 883), codified July 30, 1947 (61 Stat. 669), and amended September 3, 1954 (68 Stat. 1233). Chapter 2 added July 31, 1970 (84 Stat. 692).

Chapter 1.—GENERAL PROVISIONS

§1. Maritime transactions and commerce defined; exceptions to operation of title.
§2. Validity, irrevocability, and enforcement of agreements to arbitrate.
§3. Stay of proceedings where issue therein referable to arbitration.
§4. Failure to arbitrate under agreement; petition to United States court having jurisdiction for order to compel arbitration; notice and service thereof; hearing and determination.
§5. Appointment of arbitrators or umpire.
§6. Application heard as motion.
§7. Witnesses before arbitrators; fees; compelling attendance.
§8. Proceedings begun by libel in admiralty and seizure of vessel or property.
§9. Award of arbitrators; confirmation; jurisdiction; procedure.

CHAPTER 1.—GENERAL PROVISIONS

§1. "Maritime Transactions" and "Commerce" Defined; Exceptions to Operation of Title

"Maritime transactions," as herein defined, means charter parties, bills of lading of water carriers, agreements relating to wharfage, supplies furnished vessels or repairs of vessels, collisions, or any other matters in foreign commerce which, if the subject of controversy, would be embraced within admiralty jurisdiction; "commerce," as herein defined, means commerce among the several States or with foreign nations, or in any Territory of the United States or in the District of Columbia, or between any such Territory and another, or between any such Territory and any State or foreign nation, or between the District of Columbia and any State or Territory or foreign nation, but nothing herein contained shall apply to contracts of employment of seamen, railroad employees, or any other class of workers engaged in foreign or interstate commerce.

§2. Validity, Irrevocability, and Enforcement of Agreements to Arbitrate

A written provision in any maritime transaction or a contract evidencing a transaction involving commerce to settle by arbitration a controversy thereafter arising out of such contract or transaction, or the refusal to perform the whole or any part thereof, or an agreement in writing to submit to arbitration an existing controversy arising out of such a contract, transaction, or refusal, shall be valid, irrevocable, and enforceable, save upon such grounds as exist at law or in equity for the revocation of any contract.

§3. **Stay of Proceedings Where Issue Therein Referable to Arbitration**

If any suit or proceeding be brought in any of the courts of the United States upon any issue referable to arbitration under an agreement in writing for such arbitration, the court in which such suit is pending, upon being satisfied that the issue involved in such suit or proceeding is referable to arbitration under such an agreement, shall on application of one of the parties stay the trial of the action until such arbitration has been had in accordance with the terms of the agreement, providing the applicant for the stay is not in default in proceeding with such arbitration.

§4. **Failure to Arbitrate Under Agreement; Petition to United States Court Having Jurisdiction for Order to Compel Arbitration; Notice and Service Thereof; Hearing and Determination**

A party aggrieved by the alleged failure, neglect, or refusal of another to arbitrate under a written agreement for arbitration may petition any United States district court which, save for such agreement, would have jurisdiction under Title 28, in a civil action or in admiralty of the subject matter of a suit arising out of the controversy between the parties, for an order directing that such arbitration proceed in the manner provided for in such agreement. Five days' notice in writing of such application shall be served upon the party in default. Service thereof shall be made in the manner provided by the Federal Rules of Civil Procedure. The court shall hear the parties, and upon being satisfied that the making of the agreement for arbitration or the failure to comply therewith is not in issue, the court shall make an order directing the parties to proceed to arbitration in accordance with the terms of the agreement. The hearing and proceedings, under such agreement, shall be within the district in which the petition for an order directing such arbitration is filed. If the making of the arbitration agreement or the failure, neglect, or refusal to perform the same be in issue, the court shall proceed summarily to the trial thereof. If no jury trial be demanded by the party alleged to be in default, or if the matter in dispute is within admiralty jurisdiction, the court shall hear and determine such issue. Where such an issue is raised, the party alleged to be in default may, except in cases of admiralty, on or before the return day of the notice of application, demand a jury trial of such issue, and upon such demand the court shall make an order referring the issue or issues to a jury in the manner provided by the Federal Rules of Civil Procedure, or may specially call a jury for that purpose. If the jury find that no agreement in writing for abitration was made or that there is no default in proceeding thereunder, the proceeding shall be dismissed. If the jury find that an agreement for arbitration was made in writing and that there is a default in proceeding thereunder, the court shall make an order summarily directing the parties to proceed with the arbitration in accordance with the terms thereof.

§5. **Appointment of Arbitrators or Umpire**

If in the agreement provision be made for a method of naming or appointing an arbitrator or arbitrators or an umpire, such method shall be followed; but if no method be provided therein, or if a method be provided and any party thereto shall fail to avail himself of such method, or if for any other reason there shall be a lapse in the naming of an arbitrator or arbitrators or umpire, or in filling a vacancy, then upon the application of either party to the controversy the court shall designate and appoint an arbitrator or arbitrators or umpire, as the case may require, who shall act under the said agreement with the same force and effect as if he or they had been specifically named therein; and unless otherwise provided in the agreement the arbitration shall be by a single arbitrator.

§6. **Application Heard as Motion**

Any application to the court hereunder shall be made and heard in the manner provided by law for the making and hearing of motions, except as otherwise herein expressly provided.

§7. **Witnesses Before Arbitrators; Fees; Compelling Attendance**

The arbitrators selected either as prescribed in this title or otherwise, or a majority of them, may summon in writing any person to attend before them or any of them as a witness and in a proper case to bring with him or them any book, record, document, or paper which may be deemed material as evidence in the case. The fees for such attendance shall be the same as the fees of witnesses before masters of the United States courts. Said summons shall issue in the name of the arbitrator or arbitrators, or a majority of them, and shall be signed by the arbitrators, or a majority of them, and shall be directed to the said person and shall be served in the same manner as subpoenas to appear and testify before the court; if any person or persons so summoned to testify shall refuse or neglect to obey said summons, upon petition the United States court in and for the district in which such arbitrators, or a majority of them, are sitting may compel the attendance of such person or persons before said arbitrator or arbitrators, or punish said person or persons for contempt in the same manner provided on February 12, 1925, for securing the attendance of witnesses or their punishment for neglect or refusal to attend in the courts of the United States.

§8. Proceedings Begun by Libel in Admiralty and Seizure of Vessel or Property

If the basis of jurisdiction be a cause of action otherwise justiciable in admiralty, then, notwithstanding anything herein to the contrary the party claiming to be aggrieved may begin his proceeding hereunder by libel and seizure of the vessel or other property of the other party according to the usual course of admiralty proceedings, and the court shall then have jurisdiction to direct the parties to proceed with the arbitration and shall retain jurisdiction to enter its decree upon the award.

§9. Award of Arbitrators; Confirmation; Jurisdiction; Procedure

If the parties in their agreement have agreed that a judgment of the court shall be entered upon the award made pursuant to the arbitration, and shall specify the court, then at any time within one year after the award is made any party to the arbitration may apply to the court so specified for an order confirming the award, and thereupon the court must grant such an order unless the award is vacated, modified, or corrected as prescribed in sections 10 and 11 of this title. If no court is specified in the agreement of the parties, then such application may be made to the United States court in and for the district within which such award was made. Notice of the application shall be served upon the adverse party, and thereupon the court shall have jurisdiction of such party as though he had appeared generally in the proceeding. If the adverse party is a resident of the district within which the award was made, such service shall be made upon the adverse party or his attorney as prescribed by law for service of notice to motion in an action in the same court. If the adverse party shall be a nonresident, then the notice of the application shall be served by the marshal of any district within which the adverse party may be found in like manner as other process of the court.

§10. **Same; Vacation; Grounds; Rehearing**

In either of the following cases the United States court in and for the district wherein the award was made may make an order vacating the award upon the application of any party to the arbitration—

(a) Where the award was procured by corruption, fraud, or undue means.

(b) Where there was evident partiality or corruption in the arbitrators, or either of them.

(c) Where the arbitrators were guilty of misconduct in refusing to postpone the hearing, upon sufficient cause shown, or in refusing to hear evidence pertinent and material to the controversy; or of any other misbehavior by which the rights of any party have been prejudiced.

(d) Where the arbitrators exceeded their powers, or so imperfectly executed them that a mutual, final, and definite award upon the subject matter submitted was not made.

(e) Where an award is vacated and the time within which the agreement required the award to be made has not expired the court may, in its discretion, direct a rehearing by the arbitrators.

§11. **Same; Modification or Correction; Grounds; Order**

In either of the following cases the United States court in and for the district wherein the award was made may make an order modifying or correcting the award upon the application of any party to the arbitration—

(a) Where there was an evident material miscalculation of figures or an evident material mistake in the description of any person, thing, or property referred to in the award.

(b) Where the arbitrators have awarded upon a matter not submitted to them, unless it is a matter not affecting the merits of the decision upon the matter submitted.

(c) Where the award is imperfect in matter of form not affecting the merits of the controversy.

The order may modify and correct the award, so as to effect the intent thereof and promote justice between the parties.

§12. **Notice of Motions to Vacate or Modify; Service; Stay of Proceedings**

Notice of a motion to vacate, modify, or correct an award must be served upon the adverse party or his attorney within three months after the award is filed or delivered. If the adverse party is a resident of the district within which the award was made, such service shall be made upon the adverse party or his attorney as prescribed by law for service of notice of motion in an action in the same court. If the adverse party shall be a nonresident then the notice of the application shall be served by the marshal of any district within which the adverse party may be found in like manner as other process of the court. For the purposes of the motion any judge who might make an order to stay the proceedings in an action brought in the same court may make an order, to be served with the notice of motion, staying the proceedings of the adverse party to enforce the award.

§13. **Papers Filed with Order on Motions; Judgment; Docketing; Force and Effect; Enforcement**

The party moving for an order confirming, modifying, or correcting an award shall, at the time such order is filed with the clerk for the entry of judgment thereon, also file the following papers with the clerk:

(a) The agreement; the selection or appointment, if any, of an additional arbitrator or umpire; and each written extension of the time, if any, within which to make the award.

(b) The award.

(c) Each notice, affidavit, or other paper used upon an

application to confirm, modify, or correct the award, and a copy of each order of the court upon such an application.

The judgment shall be docketed as if it was rendered in an action.

The judgment so entered shall have the same force and effect, in all respects, as, and be subject to all the provisions of law relating to, a judgment in an action; and it may be enforced as if it had been rendered in an action in the court in which it is entered.

§14. **Contracts Not Affected**

This title shall not apply to contracts made prior to January 1, 1926.

REGIONAL OFFICES

BOSTON, Richard M. Reilly
William F. Lincoln
294 Washington Street

CHARLOTTE, John A. Ramsey
3235 Eastway Drive

CHICAGO, Charles H. Bridge, Jr.
230 W. Monroe Street

CINCINNATI, Philip S. Thompson
2308 Carew Tower

CLEVELAND, Earle C. Brown
215 Euclid Avenue

DALLAS, Helmut O. Wolff
1607 Main Street

DETROIT, Harry R. Payne, II
1035 City National Bank Building

GARDEN CITY, N.Y., Ellen Maltz-Brown
585 Stewart Avenue

HARTFORD, J. Robert Haskell
37 Lewis Street

LOS ANGELES, Tom Stevens
2333 Beverly Boulevard

MIAMI, Joseph A. Fiorillo
2451 Brickell Avenue

MINNEAPOLIS, Charlotte Neigh
1001 Foshay Tower

NEW BRUNSWICK, N.J., Patrick Westerkamp
96 Bayard Street

NEW YORK, Robert E. Meade
140 West 51st Street

PHILADELPHIA, Arthur R. Mehr
1520 Locust Street

PHOENIX, Paul A. Newnham
222 North Central Avenue

PITTSBURGH, John F. Schano
Two Gateway Center

ROCHESTER, N.Y.
36 West Main Street

SAN DIEGO, John E. Scrivner
530 Broadway

SAN FRANCISCO, William B. Allender
690 Market Street

SEATTLE, Neal M. Blacker
810 Third Avenue

SYRACUSE, Deborah Ann Brown
731 James Street

WASHINGTON, Garylee Cox
1730 Rhode Island Avenue, N.W.